Witches in Wonderland

a poetic adventure

Amanda L. Ball

Witches in Wonderland
a poetic adventure
Written and Published by
Amanda L. Ball

First Edition
Paperback ISBN: 979-8-9949807-0-5
Hardcover ISBN: 979-8-9949807-1-2
eBook ISBN: 979-8-9922822-9-0

For permission requests, please contact the author at:
contact@digitalmedleys.com

Book cover image illustrated by Fiverr designer
Full book cover designed by Amanda L. Ball

· · — ·✶· — · ·

For more content, follow the author's work on social media:
@echoendlessmind

https://digitalmedleys.com

To all of the animals I have loved and cared for. You have always given me purpose.

To my soul dog, Pinguin; you saved me from myself, and I will miss you deeply forever.

To the women who were almost drowned by other women.

To the women burned by toxic men.

May no one ever underestimate you again.

Find the women who get you. Find the women who protect you.

Most importantly, find yourself.

Pinguin

The day you departed
shattered my world,
my life no longer
revolved around yours.

You gave me purpose
every single day,
especially when I wanted
to just hide away.

You snuggled up on me
when I was sad;
you nestled into me
each night in bed.

I was your safety
and you were mine,
promising to always
protect your life.

I almost lost you
a year before;
I still can't fathom how
I brought you back to me.

You were always my light
at the end of every tunnel,
my guiding star leading me
to my purpose.

Loving you has been
my greatest joy yet;
your soul will always be
one I won't forget.

I carry you with me
etched into my skin,
and I will miss you
endlessly
until I take my last breath.

"It's just a dog"
some might say,
but you were my hero
in every single way.

May we all, one day, know freedom and love,
no longer battling the evil of the world.

· · — · ✳ · — · ·

We have been fighting for peace for so long,
I'm afraid I wouldn't recognize it if it ever arrived.

· · — · ✳ · — · ·

I am connected to the Universe through
all of the animals I have loved.

· · — · ✳ · — · ·

May the wonderland you create for yourself
be one you never want to escape from.

Adventure Guide

Dear Reader,

I wanted this book to encapsulate everything I am—who I once was, the madness I journeyed through, and the power and magic I discovered within myself along the way.

I have loved stories and books since I was a little girl. I wanted to weave this poetic adventure into a story of childhood fables and nursery rhymes, reimagined for the middle-aged adults who may be journeying through a transformation as I have done recently.

I forgot about the magic that comes with being a child for a while. It's a shame, really, that we are expected to "grow up" by a certain age. They took away our picture books, made us feel weird if we sleep with stuffed animals, told us we're crazy for believing in a fantasy. They may never stop telling us what to do while their capitalist world strips our magic away. And so, I am here to reclaim it; that is my mission.

While some of this adventure is inspired by my own life, it is also an insight into my mind—the social justice warrior, the heart three sizes too big, the empathy that boils over within me, and even the scars I once attempted to bury, now visible in my words; and a call for us all to remember we are not alone in this adventure called life.

As in Alice's story, we are forced into a world of confusion where change is never-ending. But Alice also learned to embrace the quirks in life—the odd creatures she meets, the madness we all keep, and to keep on her journey no matter how strange it may be. And on the other side, we learn who we are truly meant to be…and we embrace it fully.

I hope you find your own meaning within these words. And I hope along the way, they may help you to heal, to hope, to laugh, to find joy, and to never stop dreaming or believing in magic. Never stop reaching for your own fairytale ending. And don't forget to enjoy the strange and wondrous journey.

♡ Amanda

12

The Dream Witch: Wickedly Ever After

Now I lay me
down to sleep,
my soul to rest,
so please don't weep.

I battled demons
and almost drowned.
What I had lost
could not be found.

I walked galaxies,
I fought the dragons—
those I could see, and
those hidden in shadows.

Fueled by fire
inside my soul,
my light almost out,
no longer feel whole.

Going to bed each night
manifesting a dream land
that I could fall into,
not to awaken again.

A peaceful slumber—
all I craved,
not this hustle,
this weight,
the burdens,
the graves.

Just like Alice,
I kept awakening
knowing that the magic
exists
in another place,
on another plane.

Finding my escape—
getting lost in a book,
turning pages too fast
to get to the good.

I want to read the ending,
I want to know the answers.
I don't want the hardship,
the fighting,
the distance.

I just wanted the
happy ever after.

Instead, I found
the haunted woods,
the bears in houses
I sought for food.

I met the wolves
who bore their teeth,
waiting for their time to
strike—
to take the meat.

I saw them blow
the houses down—
those made of straw,
not rock or stone.

I saw them laugh
as the piggies scattered—
as they screamed, and bled,
as their lives shattered.

And the wolves
built castles—
such powerful structures,
while they threw
the piggies morsels,
with no paid lunches.

I walked the road—
made of yellow brick.
I danced with lions,
with tigers,
with bears…
I allowed them to
guide me
into their lairs.

I begged to see
behind the curtain;
I pleaded,
I wished,
I hoped,
and I screamed.

I cursed the man
inside the moon—
his face a reminder
of a long ago youth.

A little girl
grown up too soon.

I searched for the witches
inside the forests—
offered to lure the children,
so they could teach
while I learn.

I basked under the moon—
I never felt freer.
I steered myself
toward fun…
and danger.

I made deals with the devil,
and met the underworld
goddess—
she had it all,
the beauty, the grace—
she was my karma.

I convinced the emperor
he had on fancy robes;
pulled him into my spell,
only to leave him,
unclothed.

I fought alongside
Robin in his hood—
taking from the rich
to give to the poor.

I fed the starving children,
while I cursed evil men.
I saved all the creatures,
while I hurt some close
friends.

I thought those old bruises
of that long-ago girl
meant she deserved
a payback—of sorts.

I turned into the villain
staring into the mirror—
on the wall—in my tower;
believing I deserved
to hold all the power.

I weaved my web,
I lured in my victims;
I scattered my hurt
like it was seasoning.

I understood villains—
in the light—
in the dark.
I began to appreciate
their macabre art.

I hooded myself
in a silky, red robe.
I searched for my
granny
in the stars,
in the woods.

And when I needed
to find my way home,
she would protect me
from the monsters;
she would never
leave me alone.

I nuzzled up into
Papa Bear's lap,
asked him for
just one
more
story
before I take my nap.

Just one more chance
to watch them laugh
to watch them dance.

I begged to them—
please, bring me home.
Don't leave me here,
I can't do this alone.

I watched the princess
grow up too soon,
I watched the evil
lock her in her room.

In her mind
she dreamed up
a place
where dogs play
in rainbows,
where little girls'
daddies are safe.

Where kids don't
have to
grow up too soon;
where you can
always
wish on the moon.

Where genies are
brought
right out of
a lamp.

Where magic is real.

Where fireflies dance.

Where every miracle
comes from my hands.

Oh, she dreamed so big,
that long-ago girl,
of magic mermaids,
of a unicorn world.

So, if I shall not
tomorrow wake,
do know that I
am in a place
where little girls
are writing
on their beds
in their rooms.
Where little girls
sleep under the stars
inside the moon.

I'm stirring up villains,
writing the scripts
to give the next little girls
some dreams
and inspiration.

For good and evil
are the same—
on the same seesaw—
up…down…again.

And so, mama,
don't worry,
if your little girl's soul
leans a little bit dark,
a little more bold.

Your little girl has fire
deep inside her bones;
she will one day awaken
to all the power
that she holds.

And she will be okay
after you're long gone.
She will make her way—
as she's always done before.

You can rest in peace
knowing she is strong.
She has always carried
mountains—
in heels—
in the snow.

Yes, they call her a rebel,
but if you look deeper, still,
you will find that her heart
is three sizes too big.

She carries it all—
she writes it all down;
not always on paper—
some thoughts lost,
never found.

Maybe she will rise like
Gretel—
overturn the villains
to free the children.

Or maybe she will be Snow
White—
surrounded by friends—
by the forest—
by light.

Maybe she will fall,
like Ariel swooned,
in love with a man
who will give up too soon.

Or maybe she will dance
like Beauty
in love with her beast,
in love with his fury.

Maybe she will get lost,
like Rapunzel—
in her own stories,
as she's locked in her tower.

Maybe she will obey,
like Cinder-elly.
Maybe her [fairy]
godmother
will grant all her wishes.

May her prince—
who is charming—
never make her sleep
on a pea,
just to prove her worth,
just to be believed.

May she not fall into
a spinster's trap,
never fall into a deep sleep
in an unknown bear's lap.

May she explore
the seven seas.
May she bring kings
to their knees.

May she rise
more than she falls.
May she always
heed her own calls.

May she follow *every* dream.

May she become the heart
fit for a queen.

May she follow a rabbit
down into a hole.
May she not always do
what she is told.

I will plant these seeds in
their heads.
As you tuck them into bed.
Read these words
as they go to sleep.
I promise all
of their secrets
I'll keep.

I will nurture their minds
of possibilities—endless;
I will teach them of love.
I will teach them of
vengeance.

I will teach them courage—
unlike the lion;
I will teach them of
the real-life tin men—
the ones with no heart—
the ones who are lying.

I will teach them of witches
who might eat little
children—
but if you get to know them,
they're actually sweet, like a
kitten.

I will teach them of
adventures
out on their own—
not next to a man,
but next to a coven.

I will teach them that
animals
deserve more love than
humans,
but we should never forget
to help all of the children.

I may feed her a darker
tale—
of huntresses—starving—
turning predator on
the evil monsters.

Slithering through the
trees—
like a snake—
beady eyes
waiting to strike.

Of course, I'll tell them,
"not all men",
but many
many
many of them.

I will teach her to
go for the throat.
With her claws
with her teeth
with her soul.

But I will also bring her
out of the dark—
a nice, cozy place
under a blanket
by the fire.

A memory of wishing
up on the stars
and believing that she
can fly up to Mars.

Reminding her
there are no limits,
there are no milestones
or goals to hit.

The only goal
is to stay alive—
to dream of a night
filled with fireflies.

To remind her to not
grow up too soon.
To always say "yes"
to dancing under the moon.

To remind her to cherish
every laugh with a friend,
every tear,
every celebration.

To honor the moments
where she feels most alive.
To always tuck herself
in at night.

To show her that there is no
"right way";
to ensure she always
stands in her place.

To help those behind,
even if it's a little—
it's not such a burden
when you've already
had dinner.

To light up the world
with all of her fire,
with her breath,
her soul,
with her earthly desires.

To believe in a world
much better than this.
To remind her she never
has to have kids.

She can be whatever
she chooses to be—
a wise old witch,
run an apothecary.

Or that white picket fence
she can also choose—
that is, if
she really wants to.

But I will not let her forget
that her path is her own—
not mine, and not yours.

So read her the tales
of the witch who grants
wishes—
inside little girls' dreams—
not inside kitchens.

Where Alice is waiting
in a room full of cats,
surrounded by books
as she slips into her naps.

Pulled in by
a queen gone mad,
ready to chop off
every traitor's head.

I might weave fables
of chilling with caterpillars
wrapped up in their arms
when my head's a bit hazy.

This is the job of the Dream
Witch,
you see—
the girls dream what they
want,
believe what they choose to
believe.

I hope every single one
in every galaxy
in all the universes
in all the minds
in every star—
on every moon,

know that they hold their
own power
they know their own truth.

That there will always be
other girls out there
who will have what they
need.
Friends are the essence
of life, dear girl—
friends hold the key.

Love who you want,
but always lift
other girls up.
Pour into others,
but don't drain
your own cup.

If we allow them,
they will win—
pitting us against
one another
to control us again.

I am here to tell
the secrets that are
tucked away—
hidden well.

The tales of lists—
that don't exist—
of evil rich kings.

The tales of women
rising up
standing in
their power.

She may go home
each night
to slip into bed
with him

but she will always
be reminded
of who and what
she has always been.

As she closes her
lids each night,
I will greet her
in the light.

Guide her through
the forest
down the dark path
to remind her of
the witches' past.

To ensure they never forget
that long ago
witches were our friends.

Before man wrote the stories
that turned them into
crooks—
burned at the stake
for knowing their worth.

For seeing their magic
built right inside,
before we were cursed
into a menial life.

The spell can be broken,
it says in this book;
so come closer,
dear girls,
come, have a look.

Fall asleep each night
tucked in by the moon;
may you never have to
grow up too soon.

And if your soul—and
heart—
is a little bit darker,
may you always dream
wickedly
ever after.

For the mama bears.
And the witchy women.

Love,
The Dream Witch

A Magic World

It is now time
to envision a world
where all is fair and equal
for little girls

Where women are
never forced
into a life
that is worse
than the one
they always dreamed of

A world where greed
never wins
where cruelty is not
a word we understand
where the water we drink
and the air we breathe
is free from pollutants
and always free

This is not a fairytale wonderland
I'm painting a picture of
but a true possibility
if women were to rule the world

We have allowed men
to tear us all apart
for centuries now
destroying our earth

It is now time for
the caretakers and nurturers
to lead the way
for all the others

We need a world
not fueled by money
where the coins you have
mean absolutely nothing

A world where women
do not fear
to walk alone or have to
choose the bear

No child goes hungry
no bombs are dropped
onto innocent people
who just want
to survive long enough
to watch
their children grow
to live a life of their own

We wake up each
and every day
into a world filled
with anger and hate
and so many of us
just want to escape
into a far, far better place

We keep hoping for a carriage
that will whisk us away
to where magic exists
and where no laws can say
what we can do
with our own bodies
where we make our own rules
and men cannot haunt us

I am here to tell you
that magic is here
right where we are
within our own hands

We hold the power
to take back our land
from the evil greed
controlling it

We deserve a world
where we believe in magic again

So, rise up with us
as we all
march forward
and break down the walls
that have been barricading us
within a cage they think
is taming us

Remember your soul
comes from the stars
and you hold your own magic
right there in your heart

Wonderland Words

My words may be sad,
or silly, or mad;
they may be grim and dark.

They may empower
or make men cower,
and they definitely throw some sparks.

They may send you down
a rabbit hole,
have you shrinking
before you grow.

And they will
most certainly
introduce you to
characters so quirky.

No matter where
these words may take you,
I hope by the end,
you are chasing

the dreams that
you once had—
even if the journey
makes you feel a bit mad.

Stand up to the traitors,
make friends with the hearts
who show you kindness
in their deck of cards.

Help all the little ones
and others left behind,
and enjoy the parties
where you can dine

with the witchiest,
most untamed friends
who will be with you
until the very end.

Chat with the cats
inside of the tree,
as you follow the roads
that will lead

you into places
you never dreamed.
Never, ever forget
the magic you keep.

Drink Me

My words are meant to be consumed,
not locked inside pages in my room.
They are meant to guide others along,
to remind each reader they, too, belong.

Some words may leave them drowning
within their own tears,
sinking from the weight
of their troubles and fears;

though others will bring them back to the brink…
if only they drink.

As they stumble down the rabbit hole,
flailing endlessly to an end unknown,
grasping for something to hold onto,
slipping further and further into gloom,

they shall be greeted with trinkets galore—
tiny treasures to trigger memories of
sadness and haunting lore.

But words and fables can also spark
hope and purpose that we can impart
onto the madness within this world,
endless dreams of once-little girls.

And so, I offer you, reader, these fables and tales—
an adventure of sorts, down a wishing well.

May you journey ahead and stay the course,
even if things shall take a turn for the worse.

For fairytale adventures are not always happy and carefree;
they can be quite curious and even mad, you'll see.

Stories are not meant to keep locked up tight,
but to be devoured with tasteful delight.

Grab your book and turn the page,
slip into a dreamland full of rage,
and as you near the very end,
you will find yourself again.

Within the words, do not worry or overthink…

just drink.

Down the Rabbit Hole

Down, Down, Down

I am stuck inside my head again,
a dreadful place with no end;
just a long, dark tunnel of rage and dread,
sleepless thoughts filling up my head.

I drank the potion and ate the cake,
and the rabbit says I'm still late;
I didn't even get the chance
to slip the white gloves on my hands.

Always rushed and in a hurry,
no rest for the wicked,
only time to scurry.

Look through the keyhole into the garden,
my head too filled with madness to go inside and be a part of
a peaceful and calming restful place;
no, just worry, stress, and angst.

Searching for the secrets within this place,
so that I may return to a carefree space;
though, I worry no such place exists,
as my troubles never seem to end.

The rabbit is late and so am I;
the table is set for tea at nine;
but I cannot get myself dressed—
overgrown by the cake labeled "Eat this".

And so I shall cry a river of tears,
sending creatures swimming in their fear.
I do not recall signing up for this;
I only wanted a life of bliss.

But here I am, inside this hole
talking to cats and battling my soul,
as life is changing much too fast
and we cannot relive moments of the past.

We must venture on,
there is only one way out.
There is no going back
and so we must go down.

Down, down the rabbit hole.
Unfortunately, we will never know
where our journey will end;
yet, my thoughts continue to pull me in.

Since I cannot stop the fall,
I will turn these grim thoughts into art.
Here I go, sliding again,
writing stories with no end.

Mirror Mirror

Mirror, mirror above my bed,
please don't show me
all the thoughts in my head.

Cover them up
and tuck them in tight;
I do not have time for them tonight.

Mirror, mirror, why must you look
at me like that,
you already took

the beauty I saw and turned it around;
now I'm all backwards
and flipped upside down.

I wish I could tuck you away in a closet,
hide you from my eyes,
so I am no longer

bound by the images you display to me;
then I can pretend I am
someone else entirely.

Oh, mirror, mirror, in the dark,
reflecting my pain
like it's some kind of art.

It is not fair for you to judge me;
you've made me look like someone
I don't want to be.

Mirror, mirror, I hope that one day
you can show me
a different way.

Show me my potential for fulfilling my dreams,
not this tired, worn version
of a much older me.

Endless Dreaming

How tired is that woman in the mirror—
tired of all of the weight
of living in a world
full of anger, greed, and hate?

She smiles for the camera;
she pretends she carries it well,
then she locks herself up in a room
to stare into the mirror from hell.

The eyes are black and sunken in—
not visible in the pictures;
the bones are achy beneath the skin;
she hides the hideous features.

No makeup can cover the damage
created by all of the pain;
and there is not enough water
to put out all of her rage.

She is utterly exhausted
from picking up the pieces
dropped and scattered on the ground,
afraid she'll one day lose them.

Her bags are too full,
there is no more space
to carry more burdens,
to carry more pain.

The bags are ripping
at their seams,
and she's tired of stitching them
back up again and again.

Peaceful sleep and peaceful dreams
is all she truly craves,
as she rests beneath the tree
where she once played.

Within the pages of books,
she drowns her sorrows,
searching for an escape,
not sure what tomorrow

will bring her; will it be more anger?

Or will her worries
be carried away,
as she drifts into her dreams
never to wake?

Grim(m) Dreams

Grim dreams are always
haunting me,
lurking in shadows
inside of me.

The Brothers would surely
be delighted,
as their stories inspire
tales I'm writing.

Wicked fables
of witches brewing
stews of men—
not of children.

Macabre tellings
of villains captured
and thrown into
the witch's basement.

A little girl who
adorns her cloak
to trick the wolves
into her home,

who sets all of
the little piggies free,
and allows them to dine
on the wolves' meat.

For no little piggies should go hungry.

Fairytales of little girls
with hair so long and full of curls,
never doing what they're told,
like tossing down their hair for men to hold.

Always talking back
to villains,
taking back the reign
for all the women.

Haunting men
in the dark,
capturing them
on their hunt.

Inspiring the women
of the world
to tell these tales
to their little girls,

though they may need
to leave some words out;
not all are meant
to be read out loud.

The Brothers told
their own Grim(m) tales
with many lessons
to learn.

While I am writing
a Grim(mer) message
for the women—and girls—
of the world.

Since toxic men
will never read
the dark stories
that I weave,

this is the perfect
resting place
for my map
on how to be

wicked and evil
and extra witchy;
instructing women
to always fight dirty.

To not give in
to their manipulation.
He's a gaslighter?
I've got the matches.

Light them up.
Watch them burn,
if they can't give you
the respect you deserve.

Oh, sure, this book
will most certainly be banned
by all the men
in all the land,

so afraid of
corrupting children,
when *they* are the ones
who make them victims.

So, ladies, spread them
far and wide,
the fairytales of
a wicked life

amongst your coven
and your animal friends.

That is how I hope
my own story will end.

Lost in the Pages

As a child, the world is your oyster,
possibilities around every corner.

You hit those teen years—
invincible—with nothing to fear.

You slowly forget
what it was like to be a kid.

As you grow older
and the bills grow bigger,
sometimes you worry
how you'll buy dinner.

And all along,
the world moves on
as you hurt,
as you lose and mourn.

There is less time
for tea with friends,
days filled with errands—
and many with kids.

There you are just trying
to stay afloat,
wondering if this is truly
what life is about.

Some find an escape
at the bottom of a bottle,
some at the tables
rolling dice.

I find mine
inside
the pages of books
filled with words
that take me to
new heights.

Inside my dreams,
I can be
anything I like.

Nestled in the chapters,
right there within the cover,
I can find a grand adventure
like no other.

Where villains are defeated
and the killer gets caught,
and I can't stop reading
when I reach a good part.

While it may be an escape,
it's where I want to be—
getting lost in the pages
away from reality.

When I Was Just a Girl

From an early age
they taught me
I was competition—
not a friend or confidante,
just a punching bag
for their vengeance.

They stripped my own desires
straight from my innocent hands,
spread their lies,
stole my pride,
forcing mistrust I didn't yet
understand.

When I should have been enjoying
my young teenage crushes and friends,
they robbed me of those childhood dreams,
and I fear that's where I will end.

My love and joy contested,
my writings of secrets and pain—
like a thief in the night,
they were taken for her gain.

Just a young girl with hope in my heart,
my diary words used as her art
to paint a picture of me
she wanted my own friends to see.

Then she captured my crush…
and the next few—
for I was just a girl unwilling
to do what she'd do.

It was easy to take them—
after all, they're just boys,
just hitting puberty,
enchanted by an older girl.

She had already taken
others from me,
but she wanted him too,
so I'd set him free;

though, it was the lies—
the deceit—
I learned of too late.

When those you should trust
set out to destroy you,
you seek out the friends
meant to hold you.

But that girl also used me up,
got all she needed from my cup—
my goblet now empty,
my trust drained dry.

No wonder I sought refuge
in all the wrong guys.

I have spent a lifetime
unlearning the wrong lessons,
recovering from traumas, while
forgiving their transgressions.

The girls in my life
when I was just a girl
unboxed my secrets
and threw them out to the world.

I struggled with friendships—
with love—for so very long.
I couldn't trust men to stay
when other girls came along.

Those girls showed me how easy
it was to manipulate others—
and I admit I dabbled
at one time or another.

I missed out on that nurturing
you find amongst friends,
where you share your secrets
and can trust in them.

Instead, I learned some tougher skills—
lock your secrets up tight,
trust no one with your true self,
be in disguise when out in the light.

So, I turned my own self
into someone who
could fight every battle,
heal every bruise.

I learned to never ask for help—
for letting others in
would only lead to pure hell.

And I'm sure if you ask them
where my life went wrong,
there in their story,
it won't start with the harm

that they caused me
when I was just a girl,
learning about life,
discovering the world.

I lost myself along the way,
repeating wounds they gave to me.

All those hopes and dreams
of that once little girl
were stolen from her
by other girls.

It pains me to think
there are likely others
who are being knocked down
and sent to the slaughter.

No, I refuse to pass the baton
on any longer—
to any friend, sister,
or daughter.

While the girls of my childhood
wanted to see me fail,
the women surrounding me now
steady my sails.

It has taken many years
to undo what they did,
and while I choose to forgive,
I fear I'll never forget.

The Monster They Made Me

The monster inside me
is a scared little girl
who's angry at me,
angry at the world.

She once believed in a god
who never showed up,
who made her fight,
made her cry,
made her hurt.

And *someone* needed to protect her.

And so I became the villain
they thought me to be.
The one filled with anger
as I let out my screams.

I bottled it up
for too many years,
and as the bottle cracked,
out spilled my fears.

I had no guidance
for how to tame my demons;
so, instead, I danced
with them quite sweetly.

They comforted me
in my time of need
when no one else
was holding me.

All the pain inside of me
was too much to keep hiding,
and so, I let them all see.

In time, I finally learned to be
the monster that
they made me.

Goodbye, Cruel World

Life is flashing
before my eyes,
as my body drains
and I slowly die.
I choose to focus
on the happier times,
not the struggles
and pain wept
from my eyes.

I see the flowers
I once picked,
the wishes made
from a dandelion stick,
not the anger
and regret,
but the joyful moments
I could never forget.

We are forced to breathe,
forced to live,
though not enough people
are helping the kids.
We are forced to fight
instead of thrive;
truly, what kind of life
is this?

With my dying words,
my dying breath,
I say goodbye to a
cruel world I won't miss.

Lights Off

This light of mine
I keep tucked inside
buried within
my insecurities

To help guide others
I let it shine,
hiding it again
when it's *my* time

And so, I don't rise

Instead, I find
it easier
more comfortable
to give it away,
not saving anything
for myself—
the battery out;
drained

And it makes me feel
a little insane—
keeping all my pain
inside the dark,
refusing to impart
the weight onto others

And so, I seek my own
comfort

And my light dims,
only a flicker now
as I drown
deeper into the depths
within a wasteland
nobody wants to dig into—
a hole
long ago closed

The light no longer
penetrates,
the darkness cannot
escape,
and so I wait
(im)patiently
longingly

Though I am getting weak

And I can no longer see
as the power goes out

Lights off

And there is no breaker box

Legacy

Forced to the earth,
forced to breathe,
expected to leave
a legacy.

Some days I forget to eat.

Watching everyone
going places,
building empires,
embracing changes.

Some days I don't even walk outside.

Exercise.
Diets.
Comparing each other.

Latest fashion.
New stream.
Trying to be one another.

Some days I don't brush my hair.

All of the noise
thrown right in our faces,
berated for not complying
with society's wishes.

What is success
if you work two jobs
to make ends meet
as a single mom?

What is purpose
if you can't pay the bills
without sacrificing
your children's meals?

What is drive
if you have to walk
because you're too far
from the city bus stop?

What are goals
if you're just trying to stay afloat
while life's requirements
punch you in the throat?

Some people don't even have a home.

What is power
if the superhero doesn't win
and you have to fight the same fight
again and again?

What is freedom
if our air is not free
from pollution and toxins;
we can't even breathe.

And many do not have clean water to drink.

What is wisdom
if we can't pass the tests
they keep throwing at us
when we just want to rest?

And what is a legacy
if the marks that we leave
are erased from history,
our blood wiped clean?

I cannot keep up with these demands,
my bones are achy,
and so are my hands,
from carrying all the weight alone;
tell me, what is the purpose
of being born

when children are starving in the streets,
people dying with no heat,
and still they want us all to believe
we are enemies, you and me.

The rich and powerful are the real disease.

When I am no longer of this earth,
please plant me as a tree for my rebirth;
for maybe in another life,
I can serve the creatures just trying to get by.

They'll find rest at my trunk
and shade beneath my leaves.

Maybe my dying wish will become my legacy.

Peace:00

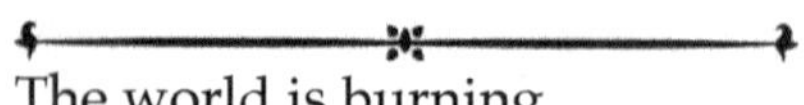

The world is burning
and there is fire in my soul.

I wish I did not know about
all the cruelties in this world.

Take me back to a simpler time,
before I was surrounded by
violence and crime.

No trust in our leaders,
no hope for the sick.

The poor are dying
while the rich get more rich.

Babies are screaming
as bombs rain down.

The viciousness of their hate
is booming and so loud.

They do not hide their crimes;
they're right in our face.

They silence the innocent
and enjoy the chase.

The cruelty is disturbing;
how much more must we take

before evil is slayed,
before we all break?

They disappear children
straight from their beds,

sending soldiers with guns
drawn to their heads.

The people with power
do nothing but watch—

just like a game show—
while we all march.

But our legs are tired,
our bones are weak.

Our feet are blistered
from the hot, hard street.

Our hearts are heavy,
our souls are worn.

Is this truly

what living is for?

My power—my voice—
is here in my words,

yearning for hope,
begging for a cure.

May we empower our neighbors
to keep standing tall;

may we protect the ones
they are coming for.

May the people on the other side
see the big picture, eyes open wide.

I know the energy of the universe
is bigger than this, older than the dirt

that our blood is seeping into,
that our tears are falling through.

Where is their god
they keep praying to?

Why would one allow
this evil through?

It will take all of the best of humanity
rising together to find our peace.

Only helping each other
will set us free.

A World of Ash

In an instant, it is all gone.

The people helping go about their day.
They clean up the room, the space.
Your job gives you a few days to grieve,
as if that's enough time to find peace.

Then the ashes come the following week.

The photos, the memories, never turn off.
The pain and the heartache are never lost.
The world expects us to move on.

What is living…
if in an instant it's all gone?

The ashes are scattered
or stuffed into a box,
turned into jewelry
or buried in dirt,
but work never stops.

How are our souls meant to heal
when deadlines are looming,
when we need that paycheck
just so we can keep breathing?

What is living…
if we are barely existing?

It is love that makes this world worth it;
still, we lose it and question if we ever deserved it.
Nothing good can ever last
when all of our joy is turned to ash,
and all we are left with is a broken past.

The future doesn't seem so bright
when loss is filling up your life.
The world, it shatters, like broken glass,
and we scurry to pick up the pieces too fast,

while others trample on our pain—
sweeping it under the rug like a grave.
And we are just expected to carry on
as if we weren't attached to something now gone.

What is living…
if it's full of loss?

My body of ash
is still living—for now;
though living ensures
we will all be returned
to the wind
or the ground.

Ghost Pain

The pain is always battling me,
though I did not ask for this duel.
It is always rattling me,
well after I've run out of fuel.

The pain in my head
leaks into my chest,
and then it spreads
into my legs.

Before I know it,
my feet are hurting,
and my achy bones
are always yearning

for just a moment
of peaceful rest
without things cracking
again and again.

When will this nightmare end?

It has been far too many years of this.

The strongest women
carry the heaviest weight
that would send weak men
to their knees.

And yet, they call *us* weak.

Let's give *them* a period for a week.

I just want my bones to rest—
to feel like a kid again,
if only for a little bit.

You may not see or believe
I have an illness;
like a ghost,
always lurking
inside my body,
like a house
that's haunted.

I fear I'll never ever stop hurting.

As I Wish Upon the Moon

Sadness creeps in
and I cut myself off
from the world again

Stress and angst
filling up my mind
and soul with pain

Struggling to see
the purpose
or the beauty

in a world
of ugly

in a world
of chaos

in a world
of sorrow
•

Maybe tomorrow
I will smile again
let the light in

but for today
I'll keep the curtains
closed

shut tight

wrapped up
out of sight
•

My heart can
no longer ache
when I can
no longer see
the world break

Stuck in this place
of misery
and longing

waiting for
belonging

Searching
for a reason
to wake
again
tomorrow
•

Another day
the same
old sun
staring down
at all
my gloom

Waiting for
the night
to fall
so that I
may wish
again
upon
the moon

Overflow

As I spew the words I say,
the words slip out in
the wrong way.

My mind is overflowing,
my heart a wrecked mess;
my soul is aching, longing,
and my body needs more rest.

Though, I am overflowing with
all the feelings in my head,
with morbid thoughts
of hopeless dread.

My coffin, lined with velvet,
waiting for me,
lowered into the ground,
turned into a tree.

My swamp witch aura
coming to rest
amongst the insects—
and dirt—
scattered into the wind.

A once imagined
happily ever after,
sealed in a jar
inside my freezer.

The spell long broken,
but it's a vision of comfort.
I have released all the longing,
no longer my burden.

Destined for this life
of woe,
like Brothers Grimm
and Edgar Allan Poe.

Though my words
may be buried with me,
they will be there forever—
my macabre legacy.

Beneath the soil
or amongst the breeze,
my soul will be etched
inside the trees.

I long to feel eternal peace.

Though, while I'm still here,
I know,
my words shall spill out
and overflow.

Breathe. Live. Death.

Life.

It ends every day.

And then it begins again.

Every day, a life snuffed out.

Every day, a new breath taken.

And yet we are still fighting
expecting to get out alive,
expecting to win
like it's all a game,
as if we remain
standing in the end.

The money hoarders
and greed goblins
stealing from others
to fill their own pockets.

The demand of others
to fit into an agenda.
The killing of children
to control land
that should never be owned.

A cycle that repeats—
a history of hate.

As soon as we take a breath,
we no longer own ourselves.

And that is why
women are forced
to produce.

More money.
More greed.

More hate.
More cruelty.

And we just go along with it—
bringing babies into a world
that will harm them
over and over again.

When will it end?

May their money burn
and their towers crumble.

May we all, one day,
love one another.

Imposter Syndrome

Here I am
dressing up again,
hiding my thoughts,
covering my skin,
ensuring no one knows
the password to get in.

On full display
for the world to see,
as I slap on a smile
to hide the parts of me
tucked within
a jumbled soul,
never knowing
where is home.

Some days are full
of happiness
and I don't need
to pretend;
but many days
I'm battling
this mind I'm
drowning in.

I write my secrets
into my stories
scattered within
the pages,
daring the world
to open them up
and discover
the puzzle
I am caged in.

Within this maze
of my life,
mysteries abound;
a walking enigma
of riddles
can always be
found
around
every corner,
but the blueprint
is there,
pressed inside the words
I have bundled
with care.

Some days I may
feel like a phony,
hiding the keys
for those to get
to know me,
but it is more fun
to plan a
scavenger hunt,
and it is only
the most worthy
who will find
all of the answers
they seek
while I hide
within my stories.

This One's for the Boys

I could tell you what not to do,
though I hope you've heard it
all before.

Boys will be boys
was meant for adventure,
not for controlling girls.

Hold her hand—
if she agrees;
always ensure
she gets home safe.

Enjoy your own
time with friends,
and remind her she
is also important.

Share your feelings,
with her and friends—
more men need to
express more emotion.

Rope in your anger,
think things out;
punching and yelling
is not allowed.

You can cry and
still be seen as strong;
strength does not come
from never showing weakness.

Your strength is in
your own ability
to control your urges,
and always love consensually.

Tell more jokes that
aren't about women's bodies;
when we can all laugh,
we find more harmony.

Let her pass you
on the street
without making her fear
or need to flee.

Understand that "No"
is a full sentence;
do not try again
when she says it.

Remember that rejection
is not an evil monster
coming to get you
or hiding in your closet.

There is no "friend zone"—
that was made up by men
who didn't get their "prize"
when she just wanted a friend.

Of course we know
you're not all bad,
but too many of you
have caused our deaths.

So, no, we do not trust you yet.

You have worth
because you are human,
so do not steal ours
because you misplaced it.

We are not meant to be
on opposite sides,
but you cannot lead
when you always think you're right.

So, please, listen a bit more tonight.

All we want
is to feel safe,
to feel respected,
to protect our space.

Our boundaries
are not negotiable;
when it comes to our bodies,
follow *our* rules.

I am certain if you navigate
this world with compassion,
you will be known as
one of the good ones.

But it takes more than what
you present to the world;
if you act out in private,
then you're still a bad dude.

And we will always see right through.

A woman's intuition
is the most powerful guide;
stop trying to trick us
into thinking you're "nice".

Our gut tells us when *that's* a lie.

This isn't a playbook
for how to get the girl.
You have to *be* a man
worthy of her.

Be the example
other young boys need;
that is how we all
live harmoniously.

It is far past time for us *all* to know peace.

Too Much to Think

I wish I had a button—
a power source—
to turn on and off
all the thoughts to sort.

A reset button
when I need to shut down,
unplug for a while
and let my thoughts drown.

Today, I'm heavy-headed,
my eyes incredibly tired,
as my mind ran through obstacles
that I thought I had retired.

I spent the night tossing
and turning in my bed,
unsafe from the demons
swirling through my head.

Will I be the victorious queen
who rises up in her power,
or the poor, helpless princess
locked inside her tower?

Will I be the hero
who saves all the children,
or trapped too soon to help—
just another victim.

The ideas are always stirring—
the woes of battles I have fought;
and a million what-ifs of a future
I thought I forgot.

I really need a switch
to turn off the light
that never shuts down—
controlling my mind.

Could I be the warrior
who saves all of her land
and all of the creatures
who deserve a helping hand?

Could I be the villain
who takes out evil men
each and every time
they harm a living being?

These are the thoughts—
the ideas, the dreams—
that I cannot break from
or rip at the seams.

Oh, my mind is a chaotic mess
with no end in sight.
And I always have a mind hangover
when I had too much to think last night.

Ghosts of My Past

Haunted hallways
haunted thoughts
creeping in
as I lock
the entry doors
and turn off
all the lights;
there they are
haunting my mind.

No rest for the wicked,
no rest for my brain,
filled with demons
that can't be contained—
prowling and howling
over my grave.

The ghosts of my past
keep torturing me
in my bed
as I sleep;
something wicked
hovering over me,
as I beg for
dreamless sleep.
But the ghosts
will never
let me be.

I draw the
blackout curtains
over the windows,
hoping they won't
know that I'm home.
I pray to the moon
to watch over me,
and pray to the crows
to chase the ghosts away.

It is an endless cycle,
a merry-go-round
of a haunted past
hunting me down.
Oh, what is a girl to do
but dance with her demons
and let the ghosts through?

Perhaps tomorrow
I'll get some rest
and stop battling the ghosts
of my past.

An Unlove Story

I just don't think it exists—
that partner who thinks like I do,
who laughs at the same silly things,
as we grow, our love does too.

I think that my heart's just different,
my vision of love a bit skewed—
not something you see in movies,
but from a story I have brewed.

It is something that doesn't exist—
something I've never seen,
just some silly thing I wrote about
that I saw in a dream.

The beast I see
would viscously protect me,
but be as soft as snow.

He'd protect my heart,
protect my mind,
and fiercely protect my soul.

He would effortlessly
support my dreams,
cheer me along
as I succeed,
be the safest space
every day,
never, ever raising
his voice at me.

It is a story of a love
that there are no words for;
one unpainted in pictures,
unsung in lyrics.

I would never have to be
someone I am not,
never have to agree
if it's not what I want.

He sees my anxiety
and is still
right
there
supporting me.

Age will not lessen
the time that we spend
smiling endlessly,
giggling like kids.

No, it is not a story
made for this world;
it is nothing I've ever
seen before.

Unfelt feelings,
unspoken words,
unlaughed laughs,
unhugged hugs.

An unloved love,
I'll continue to be;
a little unlove story
made for me.

When We Were Still Human

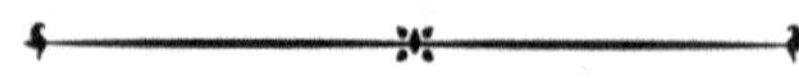

Night always felt a bit magical
looking up at the stars
nestled in the dark
not a care in the world.

Climbing trees
and skidding our knees,
unaware of the dangers,
unaware of the violence.

We shared with each other—
our toys and our laughs;
we loved one another
and had each other's backs.

We shared our discoveries
for human advancement,
to make a thriving home
for all on this planet.

But greed always takes over,
history repeats,
and all the progress we made
falls flat at our feet,
as we struggle to
pick up the pieces
left by the evil monsters
conspiring against us.

Though when evil rears
its ugly head
the people gather
and form a plan;
we see the best parts
of humanity
when love stands up
against the hate.

When we were children
it was easier to believe
that the world is good,
and villains will admit defeat
when the heroes swoop in
to save us from
ourselves again.

I long for the days
when we were still human,
when we still had hope
and we knew freedom…

Though, I am not sure humanity ever existed.

It feels like we've always been ruthless creatures.

Lilith Didn't Kneel

It started with the dawn of time,
a solo woman committing crime
against a man she disobeyed,
but Lilith refused to live that way.

She didn't bow,
she didn't kneel
to any god or man
trying to bend her will.

Banished from the garden,
she-demon as her title
she wore as a badge of honor;
vowing no man would ever own her.

Her name of Lilith, formed from "lilit",
meaning the night creature that she is,
she exclaimed,
she'd rather bleed from resistance
than rot from obedience, so that is what she did.

As the night monster,
she ventured out,
away from the garden
and the rules holding her down.

She sought out minds
that wouldn't hold her back,
building her own group
of witchy night hags.

As they crafted their own garden—
no men to impede,
they built a resistance of women
ready to bleed.

No, Lilith was never
evil, you see.
She was free.

The Expired Looking Glass

Let us stop this nonsense
of respecting our elders
just due to age,
and not due to manners.

We shall not allow
any woman or man
to outline our options
or to reprimand

the decisions and choices
we have made for ourselves;

no, we do not respect those who
judge us the way our elders do.

The generations that raised us
do not seem to approve
of the paths we have taken,
the lives that we choose.

They are trying so desperately
to hold on to control;
though they are weakening
as new generations are born.

Let us now teach children
respect should be earned;
do not trust blindly,
but do not cause harm.

We are the generations raised
on worldwide knowledge,
access to cultures and people
who do not live around us.

We are not allowing
closet doors to stay shut;
we are decorating our minds and bodies;
we are opening up

all the doors to possibilities;
we are not shaming children
for who they choose to be.

We do not have to take kindly
to people who judge us,
people who shame us,
people who blame us

for Christianity slipping away;
they need to be reminded
that religious freedom
shall not be denied here.

More hair of rainbow,
more faces with jewelry,
more black clothing,
more inked up bodies.

The crowds around me
feel like home;
we are no longer hiding
who we are.

So, no, I do not respect my elders.
I respect the people who see beyond
the societal rules that tell us
where we belong.

No matter the generation,
no matter the age,
I respect those who
respect my space.

A Hauntingly Haunt

A whisper in the dark
a chill in the air
secrets on the wind
left vulnerable and bare.

Bare feet sprinting
across gravel and dirt,
running from people
stealing my worth.

Worthless soles
on worthless feet,
worthless souls
feeding on me.

My trauma chasing me
cutting through the branches,
piercing skin
limiting my chances.

Chance or fate,
a twist in the story—
a grave is dug
in the cemetery.

Cementing my worry
as I peer inside—
will I defeat the monster…
or will it bury me alive?

Returning Home

When I die, please return me to the fire—
where I was born in the middle of April.

Take my ashes, and spread them around—
out in the ocean and buried underground.

Ensure some are sent back into the wind—
returned to the Universe where I began.

I shall live on forever as my remains are connected
back to the water, the earth, the wind, and the fire.

My Dreams

Many a man
will chase fortune
or fame;
many believe
success
can be gained
by making more
money
by winning more games.

I am choosing
a life that is free
from stipulations,
laws, and greed.
I am only
seeking comfort
and peace.
My own little fortress
amongst the trees.

I dream of a place
that I can live in,
with my own garden
of secrets hidden.
Filled with books,
filled with stories,
filled with love,
and animal companions.

I do not dream of
wealth from money;
though, if I were to have it,
I'd help the hungry.
I would share with friends,
lessen their troubles,
and we would all live happily
in our little bubble.

There is a dreamland
in a far away place,
another dimension
I hope to find one day,
where women are honored
and women are praised,
men are not evil, and
where the innocent are safe.

In my dreams
of that once-little girl,
there are no monsters
controlling the world.
She can climb any mountain,
as she dances and twirls;
she can lead the people;
she can brave any storm.

That little girl saw beauty
in everything she viewed;
she believed she could
do *anything* she wanted to do.
I don't want her to lose the wonder
that she once knew.
In my dreams,
her dreams come true.

Ellipsis…

My mind continues,
it carries on;
no thought final,
no story done…

Words always lingering
on my tongue,
within my mind,
an unwritten song…

Tales of desire,
tales of fight,
tales of rage,
and the witches' delight…

when they join
hands together,
much more powerful
when they gather…

and take back the world with their power.

Where one story ends,
another begins;
as it trails on,
the plot, it spins…

around and around
as I chase it down,
leaving behind my ellipsis
until the right words are found…

Escaping Reality

Jumping on the trampoline,
I feel so young and free again.

Catching fireflies in a jar,
playing hide and seek in the yard.

Jumping rope,
singing songs,
playing teacher
with my dolls.

Host a tea party,
invite my friends,
as we giggle over
our secrets.

Rediscovering the joy
I had as a kid,
before I knew
the world was sick.

Endless dreams
of countless possibilities.

Believing we can always
defeat our enemies.

They threw all the fairytales
right in our face,
and then wonder why
we demand more grace.

I may have watched
all the girls get pursued,
but I also saw the villains
paying their due.

I've seen dragons fall
straight from the sky,
believing that we win
when we fight.

I may not have the strength
to pull the sword from the stone,
but I can swing daggers
right at their throats.

I will not play the damsel
in her room in distress;
I will sneak in
while they rest.

The witches of the fairytales
taught me how to bake poison pastries,
how to brew potions,
how to act a little crazy.

Like Maleficent, I can turn quite quickly,
from sexy queen to evil villain.

As Little Red Riding Hood
adorns her cloak, sneaking off
to granny's home—

though, what the story
failed to mention,
is the girl knew all along
the wolf was vicious.

She lured him there
under false pretenses,
delivering the goods
in her basket.

Beauty may have chosen
to save the Beast—
after he held her captive
and caused her grief.

I may be Alice, out on her own,
adventuring out to learn a bit more,
feeling small then growing big,
talking to animals,
dreaming like a kid.

But I am no hero
and certainly no princess;
just a tired middle-aged woman
who doesn't want to do the dishes.

I choose escape inside my stories,
within the pages is where I journey.

For in the words, within the text,
I can feel like a kid again.

In a Land Not So Far Away

Once upon a time
in a land not so far away,
there lived a woman
unaware of her power.

She built her own life
in the way that she wanted;
though from the outside,
she appeared lonely in her tower.

She gave much of her time
caring for others,
as she found her own way
and made her own peace.

At times she was gentle,
nurturing the innocent;
though when the match was struck,
the fire within her released.

She didn't seek out
princes on white horses;
she did not ask to be saved,
for she was her own hero.

All the people of the palace
demanded she settle—
this world was no place for a woman
with no husband and children of zero.

Though the woman lived happily
in her cottage within the forest,
building her family of animals,
friends, herbs, and crafts.

As she enjoyed her hobbies
and kept to herself,
the kingdom set out
to accuse her of witchcraft.

For a woman should never
be so happy alone,
expected to bow to man
in her own home.

Raise the children,
say, "yes, sir",
do what you're told,
do not disturb

the men as they go about
their day;
they make the decisions
on everything.

Though, that life did not suit her;
she forged a new path,
and now the men's evil was coming…
and they'd soon experience her wrath.

She tried to be peaceful,
to be kind and give back,
but she always refused
to allow men to lay out her tracks.

And as they near closer,
she knows not if she will prevail;
though, this is her story;
this is her tale.

Chasing the Rabbit

Here I go again,
chasing something
that's never been

A wonderland,
a dreamland,
a fantasy world

A place where
all creatures wander
free from scorn

Pristine lakes and the
greenest fields,
a place where we
all can build

a life we truly adore…

not the rush of time
or the rush of deadlines

But the rabbit is always
running late,
there is no time to
clean my plate
or relish in the
dinner chat

No, time is ticking
and we can't go back

I could lie still
and let time pass,
but I prefer adventure
in the hourglass

So, I'll chase the rabbit
and stumble upon danger,
meet new creatures,
make friends with strangers

I'll set the table
in the yard for tea;
maybe the rabbit
will join me

But I shall not hasten
as quickly as he,
for I want to enjoy this
journey given to me

Make more memories,
see more sights,
and always stop to chat
with a cat at night

Watch the cows
jump over the moon,
and keep writing poetry
in my bed in my room

Though the world is mad,
I refuse to give in
to all of the cruelty
we are buried in

Instead, I will build
my own wonderland

I choose to chase the rabbit
where no book or person
is banned

Curiouser and Curiouser

Alice and the Three Witches

Alice ventured into the forest
not sure what she would find.
And to ensure she made her way back home,
she left a trail of crumbs behind.

Though Alice was familiar with these woods,
she always discovered something new,
as if magic kept revealing
secrets she could view.

As she trekked further in,
she found a tiny cottage.
She knew it was not there before,
she truly would have caught it.

A new piece to the puzzle
she had been putting together—
a map she was drawing
of places to gather
to do her bidding inside the trees;
a forest life of her own dreams.

As she neared the purple door,
she smelled scents un-smelled before,
and laughs rang out through the open windows;
Alice wondered if she was just in time for dinner.

She knocked three times and waited patiently,
hoping to be granted entry,
and as the door creaked slowly open,
three women stood, wearing aprons.

One covered in flour from head to toe,
another with jam up to her elbows,
and the third adorning a wicked grin...
as she had played some tricks on them.

They were not startled
by Alice's arrival;
it's as if they were expecting her.
And they stepped aside,
as an invite,
to allow Alice to enter.

As she looked around, Alice found
a room full of shelves and bottles.
A cauldron was brewing,
something stewing,
that made Alice's mouth water.

Books were strewn around the room,
open to recipe pages.
So many ingredient words
Alice had never heard,
and she had a lot of questions.

The women, they giggled,
as they went back to the kitchen,
leaving Alice behind.
And so, she prowled
through the house,
taking her own sweet time.

When they returned
to join her,
pointed hats were atop their heads.
And in one's hand,
a special wand,
and then the witches said,

Alice, you have come at last,
and oh, we missed you so!
We knew you'd find us again some day;
we're so glad that you are home.

Alice was bewildered,
as she was quite certain
she had not been here before,
she did not know these women.

But as they dined and ate the stew,
Alice kept learning something new,
as if old memories were returning
of a family for which she was always yearning.

And as the last drop was consumed—
of the most delicious food—
Alice discovered what she once knew…
the magic she held inside her.

21st Century Poe(t)

Let my dagger of words stab you deep
while your soul bleeds out at your feet.

Let my tangled web of words stitch up
your soul, heal the hurt.

May my words rope you in and make you
feel empowered again.

And may they touch your inner child, so
you can remember what it meant to be wild.

And may my own very wish one day come
true; it would be my victory

if I were to become the Edgar. Allan. Poe.
of the twenty-first century.

Saving Daylight

When the daylight is saved,
we feel less grey,
with shorter nights
and longer days.

When the sun is out
we don't feel so down;
night passes quick,
then it's daylight again.

But as the savings
comes to an end,
we feel that bit
of gloom set in.

And it is so easy
to forget
that night has always
been my friend.

I feel more cozy,
I feel more relaxed
when I can nestle in
with my cats.

No sunshine keeping me
way too warm,
and the moon is there—
my lucky charm.

My mind fills up
with words a-plenty
when darkness arrives
way too early.

And I can write my little heart out,
as the savings of daylight ends;
and all the stories trapped inside
can finally escape and let wonder begin.

Caterpillar Dreams

Such a hungry caterpillar
looking for its next meal,
it doesn't mind getting fat
on what it chooses to steal.

He dreams of becoming the largest
in all of the land,
where he will then demand
mushroom stew
in a bowl of leaves,
sprinkled on top with
flower seeds
and fruits
and roots
and stems…
a dreamy concoction
he'll only share with
stuffed friends.

Oh, he ate and he ate
until nothing was left—
a leafless garden,
not even a stem.

His friends felt so rich
dining with him,
with no concern
for those in the storm.

And as the meeker caterpillars
sought shelter in their cocoons,
the selfish ones above
would meet their death quite soon.

Now too fat to fit inside,
for all the food they stole and ate
locked them out of their cocoon nests—
a much safer space.

And so, the storm rolled on through,
flooding out the garden,
washing all the rich grub away,
while not one cocoon had fallen.

Tucked away for many days,
the meek caterpillars, they sleep;
they would one day bloom—in due time—
to butterflies,
in their caterpillar dreams.

Weird and Whimsical

Floating
Flying
Frolicking

as whimsical as can be

Fairies
Fireflies
Flickering

lighting up the sky for me

Weird
Whimsical
Witchy

the best ones always are

Wild
Feral
Rebels

I never have to look too far

Outcasts
Misfits
Untamed

we never do what we're told

Strong
Resilient
Powerful

they are always the most bold

Lovers
Nurturers
Supporters

caring for all they know

Daring
Courageous
Determined

chasing all their goals

All the whimsical weirdos
who I've come to know and love
are the most magical creatures
in the entire fucking world

Hey Tweedle Tweedle

Hey, Tweedle Tweedle
give me a riddle.
A joke will also do.

For I need a laugh,
so please distract
me from my own gloom.

No need to battle
over a rattle,
the crows will give you fright.

Please come join me
for some mad chattery
so that I can forget tonight.

I've grown too fast
and now my back
is aching, as is my neck.

Feeling older
and much slower,
my mind is such a wreck.

Hey Tweedle Tweedle,
help me find a needle
buried in this haystack.

I need a distraction,
a task of action,
before I completely crack.

Love at First Sight

Do you believe
in love at first sight,
staring at love
right in the eyes?

Or is it so
that true love
must grow,
and only time
ensures
that you know?

It was so easy
as a kid
to believe in
true love's kiss.

But then you hit
middle age,
no love has come,
and you're a bit grey.

It's not that
you're lonely,
you are surrounded
by love
from friends
and animals
and the souls
up above.

Though, that *true* love
feels so far away
when you get older
in a world of hate.

It is hard to trust
who is true,
what is real,
who are you.

Deceit and lies
thrown in your face,
as you struggle to see
if love has a place.

Ghosts are endless,
disappearing,
and reappearing
on a whim.

It is quite frustrating
not knowing what
could have been.

I do believe that
romantic love
needs plenty of time
to bloom.

But I do believe
in love at first sight
when I meet a new animal
to bring home.

The endless love
of our furry companions
is all I truly need.

And if true love's kiss
were to meet my lips,
it could end in tragedy.

The Spell Jar

A pinch of black salt
for protection,
a dab of cinnamon
for love.

Lavender and
amethyst
for peace
and happiness.

Coffee, for power,
glitter for celebration,
a bay leaf for prosperity;
don't throw in with hesitation!

Keep adding each ingredient
and others of your choosing.
With the magic in your bones,
the whole universe is your oyster.

Witch

I am not a witch because I worship a so-called devil.
I am not a witch because I have psychic powers.
I am not a witch because of my wicked heart—
that part
is just coincidence.

I am a witch because of my connection
to the Universe and Mother Nature.
While I may mix up some spells here and there,
I am a witch because I am aware.

According to religion, evil started long ago,
well before woman (and man) walked this earth.
The gods, they battled one another…
apparently even *they* needed to compare whose dick was bigger.

And as I grew and learned more of the world,
I saw the evil taking over us.
There is no living in harmony
when we are being bombed by cruelty.

So, I chose a new path ahead,
not filled with gods, or devils, or religion.
I searched for the like-minded women
who could teach me the ways of the coven.

I am a witch because evil exists,
and this world needs more fighting against it.
And I am certain that I have always had
a bit of magic inside my soul, bones, and hands.

We are connected to all that has ever been,
tucked away in the stars, moving on the wind.
I don't have all the answers, though I'm always searching.
I choose to be a witch who is always learning.

The Key(hole) to My Heart

My little dark heart
crafts beautiful art.

It may be covered in thorny brambles
and sometimes torn into shambles;
though it may be locked,
the key is not lost.

Behind the bars, in its dark cage,
it writes down words that can raise
the hopeless souls into their power
and make weak, evil men cower.

It is not so lonely here inside;
I've decorated my space with pride.
This little dark heart of mine
swells with love all the time.

Though in this castle it is locked within,
it bathes in darkness in its coffin,
only a keyhole to peek into
so you may see inside the room.

What you will find
when you peer deep inside
is a messy history,
but you will also see
the kindness shown
to strangers unknown,
the assistance given
to helpless children.
You will see the love bestowed
onto frightened animals with no home.

And there inside my dark heart
you will find my favorite part—
the wishes I have made for friends,
the endless love I have for them.

Though my heart may be locked up,
the key is easy to find, if only you look;
for all the answers that you seek
are there in the hole inside of me.

Slowly it will be filled back up,
as my heart recovers from the damage done
by the chaos in my past;
though, healing doesn't happen fast.

You don't need potions to make you small
to climb inside my barricaded walls.
You only need to look inside
the keyhole of my heart to find
the puzzle pieces I have scattered
amongst the stories I have crafted.

Word Nerd

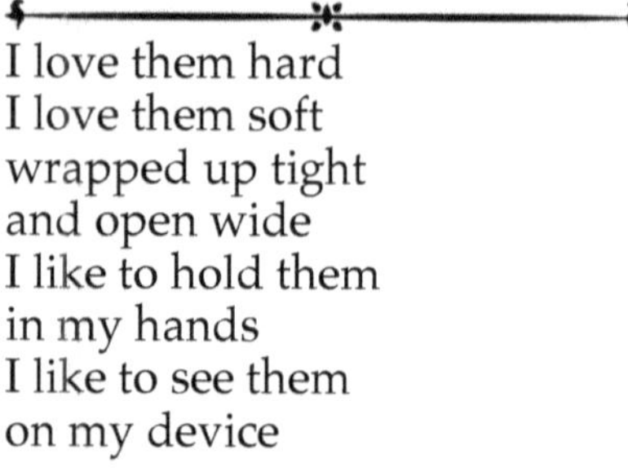

I love them hard
I love them soft
wrapped up tight
and open wide
I like to hold them
in my hands
I like to see them
on my device

I like them short
I like them long
I like them funny
and in a song
Sometimes resting
on the tip of my tongue
I like them old
I like them young

I like them tumbling
out of my lips
falling out of my hands
as they slip

onto the pages
into the books
devouring
all the words

Books and words
have become my life

I'm just a little word nerd
reading and writing
all day and all night

Lollipops and Coffee Beans

Lollipops and Coffee Beans,
all the treats of my dreams.
I bought some at the farmer's market,
but on the way home, I dropped it.
A little witch, she picked it up
and asked if I had more to share.
Though I did not plan to give away
the treats I bought for me that day.
She offered me a penny,
but I shook my head, no.
I cannot accept her money;
after all, she has no home.
And so, I left her with my basket
with all my favorite treats.
That's just what you do
when you have enough food;
and I can always get more sweets.

Psycho Kitty

Soft kitty, psycho kitty
little paws with knives.
Warm kitty, heavy kitty,
living your nine lives.

Psycho kitty, psycho kitty
wreaking havoc in my house.
Precious kitty, silly kitty
meow, meow, meow.

•

Psycho cat, psycho cat
what am I feeding you
to make you act belligerent
you tiny little psycho?

Psycho cat, psycho cat
it's all your fault
that I am covered in scratches
from your little dagger claws.

Red Hat, Blue Hat

Red hat, red hat,
coming toward me,
trying to tell me
who to be.

Wanting to know
what's under my clothes
so they can tell me
which bathroom to use.

Harming their partners—
so much abuse;
never, ever letting
a woman choose.

So pro-life,
they're willing to kill
any woman who doesn't
bend to their will.

Red hat, red hat
flashing their guns,
shooting up schools…
and their own fans.

Stealing from the hungry
to feed the rich,
not even realizing
they're being used by them.

Using their god
to spew their hate,
to control their followers,
and to berate.

Red hat, red hat,
swinging their tiny dicks
as they rev their engine
on their fucking trucks.

Red hat, red hat,
they don't know
what loyalty means,
even turning on their own.

They don't know kindness,
they don't know love,
no space for compassion,
no room to grow.

Stuffed in their hats,
giving Nazi salutes.
At least you're not hiding…
so we can find you.

You call us woke—
all you do is snooze.
And snowflakes can form
a blizzard too.

Red hat, red hat,
never blue.
We don't need hats
to prove shit to you.

Alice Had a Little Rabbit

Alice had a little rabbit,
his fur as black as coal,
and every night that Alice slept,
off the rabbit would go.

He'd hop all night within the forest
to meet the other hares,
never late for important dates,
and never feeling scared.

Alice taught him to have no fear
as he hopped along,
even when a predator was near
he calmed himself with song.

And why is the rabbit so black, you ask,
instead of white like snow?
For the same reason witches prefer black cats;
I was sure that you would know.

Black rabbits can hide within the night
and carry the witches' letters;
with the cats and crows in tow,
Alice may retrieve what she is owed
across the land from all of her debtors.

Deck of Cards

The deck is stacked against me,
I have no luck to my name.
My poker face is getting rusty,
and I'm tired of these games.

The diamonds glaring back at me;
all I have is a pair of threes,
and that is not enough to win
this poker game that I'm playing in.

And so I fold,
again and again.

A new deck has been shuffled;
I'm feeling better about my chances,
and I place my bet down,
as the dealer lays the hands out.

It is quite a mix of suits,
though I do have some spades close in number.
If I could just get *one* more card,
this straight would come together.

But I am outnumbered—with lesser coins,
and so I fold again,
waiting for a new game to start,
anticipating my next hand.

Oh, this one is more like it—a flush of clubs;
although, they are the smallest numbers,
with time, it is apparent
my hand is getting stronger.

Tough luck, again; the four queens win,
and I am down to my last token.
I have to go all-in, afraid
I'll be dealt a pair of jokers.

I ask the dealer, please shuffle better;
this deck is not stacked in my favor,
and I am losing ground, as I turn
out my pockets, more coins are found.

That feels like a small stroke of fortune,
though it may not seem like much;
I must take even the smallest wins;
as long as I have *something*, I can't give up.

And as the cards are spread around,
dealt to each player's hand,
I empty out my pockets for
my final go all-in.

It is the end—do or die,
though I feel I'll never win.
But alas, as the cards are passed,
it's as if I have always been

shuffling—and struggling—
destined for this game of cards.
Finally, I win the pot of gold
with my royal flush of hearts.

Wandering Mind of Wonder

My wondering mind
wanders,
it gets a little lost,
in its corners, ghosts,
hidden in the dark.
The past, the present,
the future
all bundles into one,
as my wandering mind
wonders
what more is there to come.
The wonders of the world
can feel too much
for a wandering mind;
and if I ponder
too much on this wonder
I just might find
the answers I am seeking,
though, it often feels
like I am blind
to all the wonders
that have transpired
as I have wandered
through this life.
And so, I wonder
if I dare to wander
just a bit longer, still.
For there may be wonders
to discover
on my wandering journey
before my life is fully fulfilled.

Mushroom A(M)aze

Ring around the mushrooms
through this mushroom maze.
A life of laughter and joy
is all that I crave.
Each mushroom connected
by an underground system,
sharing their resources,
building their friendships.
The plants discovered
a long time ago,
that we all have a fighting chance
if we help each other grow.
They're delivering nourishment
to their neighbors,
swapping their nutrients
to save for later.
They bask in the sun,
not battling each other,
not hoarding all
of the food and water.
They send their signals
to warn of danger,
so all the plants may fend
off any evil traitors.
The mushrooms we see
above the surface
are spreading more spores
to grow more abundance.
They aren't taking count
of who owns what;
they simply spread the love—
no need to flaunt.
In this Wood Wide Web
they built long ago,
they've made it their mission
to protect their home.
They nurture each other
and nurture us, too.
A little underground maze,
the amazing mushrooms.

Much Muchier

Be too much.
Be too you.
When you think you've reached your max potential,
add a little extra sparkle to the mixture.

Never water yourself down
for anyone;
you can't be too loud
or have too much fun.

Be too silly.
Be too ambitious.
Be too proud
of all your achievements.

Be too loving.
Be too kind.
Be too amazing.
Be too alive.

When they say you're too much,
I believe
you can be much muchier—
much more of everything.

Do not lose your muchness.
Do not lose that spark
that makes you You—
much muchier by far.

Black Cat, Black Cat

Black cat, black cat,
what do you see
staring out of the void
looking at me?

Black cat, black cat,
the darkest shadow,
the tiniest monster
with the sharpest daggers.

Black cat, black cat,
hair dark as night
on the darkest eve
with no moonlight.

Black cat, black cat,
you're not unlucky,
you don't bring curses,
but love a-plenty.

Black cat, black cat,
just a tiny panther
ruling our home
with all your bad manners.

Black cat, black cat,
stop yelling at me;
you've already been fed,
you cannot be hungry.

Black cat, black cat,
my lucky charm,
lying on my chest
keeping me warm.

Black cat, black cat,
it's plain to see,
you are *not* a void,
as you complete me.

Life is but a Dream

Roll, roll, roll the dice;
what life will I lead?

[Will I be kind,
and witty, and clever;
will I always be
able to weather
all of the storms
and chaos I face;
will I adventure
or stay in one place?

Will I allow the world
to break me
with all of the cruelty
and all of the anger?

Will I build the
life I envision;
will I make my enemies
my victims?

Will love always be
just out of reach;
will my friendships
last an eternity?

Will I be able to help
others in need?
May I never, ever
get buried in greed.

I hope I find comfort
in the rainy days,
knowing that new life
and hope is on the way.
I hope I enjoy
the sun on my face
and always find
a safe space
to rest my bones
when I am weary,
to never, ever
go to bed hungry.

Though we may be
born with obstacles
as soon as we take
a breath,
may we all still chase
our own desires,
choose our own path.
May we envision—
and build—
a peaceful land
with a calming stream.]

Wishfully, wishfully,
wishfully, wishfully,
life is but a dream.

Alice and the Beanstalk

As Alice walked along her path
through the enchanted woods,
she stumbled upon some fresh seeds
laid upon the dirt.

They were not buried or planted,
no one around to water and watch them grow,
and so,
Alice picked them up
and she took them home.

The seeds were planted in her garden
where all her secrets rested.
She watered them daily as she sang;
she was truly invested.

And then, one day, as she walked outside,
she saw the stalk had grown tall and wide,
a ladder that she could climb
right up into the great big sky.

Alice always loved adventure,
and this beanstalk was a beautiful picture
of all of the wonders
she could discover
if only she would brave the thunder.

As the storm was rolling in—
and every day, again and again—
it seemed the beanstalk that she grew
brought with it weather she never knew.

Although it was quite frightening,
she battled bolts of lightning
to climb the stalk
to the top
and have a look around.

As she made her way inside
of the secret house in the sky,
she was quickly greeted by
the most peculiar creature she'd ever spied.

Its eyes, surprised,
and grin, so wide,
as the creature realized
Alice was only six inches high.

Alice was not alarmed
when the giant lay down its arm,
allowing Alice to climb onto
its hand, nestled in its palm.

Alice was ecstatic with this discovery,
as was the giant, so it seemed.
They taught each other everything
that they each knew, that they each dreamed.

Alice knew that being different
was not so bad at all;
though, her giant friend
atop of this beanstalk
was too afraid
to show its face
to the great, big world.

Who could ever love a creature
who looked so peculiar—
not fitting in
with any of the people?

What life could it lead
without a true identity—
always trying to fit in,
but failing miserably?

Alice was certain she knew what to do,
so she invited the giant down to her home.
And tucked into her secret garden
outside her cottage window,
the creature constructed a palace
they could both live in near the willow.

For there was no reason for either one to be
alone on this journey through life, you see.
Through Alice's bravery—and heart for adventure—
she found more beauty than she could venture;
by daring to go where no one else had,
she discovered friendship and love down a different path.

She always loved the road less traveled.
And now she had a fierce protector—
a friend forever after.

Lisa Frankly

It is quite clear how we got here—
bright colors and stickers galore;
we were mesmerized by
the big cartoon eyes
always left wanting more.

And so, we began decorating
and coloring our bodies,
building our sticker collection slowly,
dressing them up
like a Trapper Keeper—
they make us feel less lonely.

Just like we used to
collect stuffed animals,
now we collect artwork
for our own canvas,
even when
society demands
that we cover up, frankly,
we don't give a damn.

Through Lisa's designs
we learned from her
that artwork is beauty
and can be fun
when you look different,
when you stand out,
when you mix rainbow colors
and throw them around.

Though, Lisa was not
a weirdo like us;
she actually turned
quite greedy.

I refuse to let that take
the weirdness from me
because frankly,
normies are creepy.

Feral Fall

Hot girl summer has come to an end
and now the fun can really begin.

The jack-o'-lanterns are carved,
the cats all turned black,
the firewood has been gathered,
and the leaves are all stacked
into a pile for which we can leap,
and then gather around the fire,
bundled up in cozy clothes,
where darker tales are transpired.

Oh, I live for the nights
with a chill in the air;
the nights filled with spooky
decor in my lair.

I melt all summer
and crave the days
when apples and pumpkins
fill up my space.

Oh, I'll sit in my chair
with a bowl full of treats
for all the spooky weirdos
playing tricks on me.

Fall is the time
the witch can play,
as she sings and dances
on top of graves.

And though the normies
may whisper and mock her,
she is not completely
off her rocker.

She simply enjoys
the haunt on the breeze,
wrapped in her blanket
as the feral fall queen.

A Deadly Letter

It feels quite grim
to even be writing this—
posthumous works,
is there anything worse
than words left unread
on a page—or in a screen—
not like the old days,
when words were etched
into handmade scrolls,
rolled up, sent off
out into the world
to be delivered to
waiting parties—
good news or sad—
the envelope never tells.
And so, these words
are wrapped up tight
(inside my digital device)
waiting for the passcode
to be entered…
or lost forever
in the ocean of the ether.
If these grim words
should find you soon,
you can find me resting
in my crescent room.

Butterflies and Lies

They make you think you're getting
all the fluttering butterflies,
but hidden behind their kisses
is a mouth full of lies.

They may think I've become
a hater of men,
but they've never given me
a reason to trust in them.

Their love is not real,
it's really just lust,
until they find someone younger,
or with a larger bust.

Women are not allowed to age,
not allowed to grow,
not allowed to change.

We are expected to do
everything with grace,
while men spew hate and anger
right in our face.

Then they hear the word "feminist"
and call themselves victims,
as if women don't know
what it feels like to be defenseless.

They say our emotions
prove we cannot lead,
as they punch holes in walls
and make women bleed.

So, it's not all snakes
and it's not all men,
but it's always *our* fault
when they become mad.

They think that we owe them
our bodies and time;
they demand respect
but don't know how to be kind.

It takes young girls
much too long to see
that men will manipulate
to get what they need.

You may call me a cynic,
but that's all I've seen.
So fuck butterflies,
I have my own wings.

The Night Before Solstice

'Twas the eve before solstice
and all through the night
creatures were stirring—
bats, crows, and mice.

The shortest day
and longest night,
they anticipated
with much delight.

The people were planning
for the shortest day,
for the darkest eve
as the sun slips away.

They gathered their torches
and gathered their lanterns,
prepared their cloaks
to keep warm their
skeletons.

They chopped more wood
for a fire, so toasty,
and collected marshmallows
they'd need for roasting.

They prepped the stew
and prepped the s'mores,
not knowing what the
longest night had in store.

Would it be wicked;
would it be ghoulish;
would it bring nightmares
in dreams so foolish?

Would it bring magic
back into their homes,
they wondered as they
tucked in their bones.

A Poem for the Poet

They all want to know the ending
before learning the parts in between.

Rushing through the pages,
learning absolutely nothing.

Skipping to later chapters,
missing important parts.

Reading is quite easy,
but poetry is an art.

The poet writes stories
with fewer words.

We create characters
full of yearn.

Is it a lost art
or just a lost love?

Did we get it wrong,
falling for words?

Are we all destined
to go unheard?

Like Shel, and Edgar, and Sylvia,
like Maya, and Dickinson, and Frost,
I hope the world never forgets…

If no one wants to read the poems,
who will ever read the poets?

Hallway to Hell

I'm in the hallway to hell—
not that song we all know so well—
a winding hall,
so long and dark,
but filled with comfort
in my heart.
I feel the other
deep, lost souls
who were berated
and constantly told
they would not be
accepted into their
heavenly eternity.

And so mote it be…

As I near the end of the hall—
at the end of this journey I've been on—
I hear the most joyous sounds
and see rainbows, glitter,
and thorny branches,
black paint dripping
onto the curtains.
And this hallway to hell
I've been traveling on
is no longer a dream.

I'm home.

The Itsy Bitsy Witch

The itsy bitsy witch
went out into the world
searching for the love
she hoped for since
she was a girl.

She crossed the path
of many men,
some too mean,
some too dim.

Her trust was rattled
many times,
as they kept swooping in
with their lies.

She encountered evil,
she encountered ghosts;
she lost too much time,
and she lost hope.

And so, she sought
out friendships so great—
so true and pure,
no man could compete.

And the itsy bitsy witch
healed from her past;
amongst animals and friends,
she found herself at last.

Curiouser and Curiouser

The madness we keep
is buried deep
within our bones,
within our souls

It is impossible to know
who sees us clearly;
impossible(r), still,
to show ourselves merely

as we are, and nothing more;
we conceal the curious parts
within our core

As children, we're all silly,
quirky, carefree;
and then we grow with potions
that read "Eat me"

And it's as if we forget how to be

Who are you?
Who is me?

It's as curious as can be

We forget about our
invisible friends;
we no longer see ghosts,
just toxic men

We bury our past,
forgetting we were once kids,
and no one is inviting us
out to play again

We step on all the cracks
and don't pick up the pennies,
we think we're all grown
when we enter our twenties

And so, we don't
listen to learn,
we must be right,
so we speak out of turn

We act right mad
with drinks and drugs
filling up our heads

And then we turn
another corner;
our thirties are here and we
think we're quite clever

We climb some ladders
and make more mistakes,
ruin our credit
then build it again

It's like a merry-go-round that never ends

What is credit, anyway?
This must be some mistake

It is quite curious here...

And we learn some hard lessons
and lose more we love,
and always expected to
pick ourselves right back up

The hustle and bustle
is weighing us down;
we're really starting
to feel it now—

the aches and pains,
the squeaky joints;
though we've earned
a few more credit points

There it is again—
fucking credit;
what is this shit?

More to add to
the list
that spells out
our credentials,
telling people if
we're worth it

It doesn't get much madder than this

It is quite curious
after leaving your thirties,
there is a shift
and you're all different

My mind has changed,
I'm sure of it

Not only is my
body giving up,
but this damn brain
keeps slipping up—
my thoughts all twisted
as bad as my ankle;
now I can't frolic,
prance, or prankle

(you can look it up)

They don't prepare you as a child
that one day, you'll let go your wild

It is quite curious how we're all beguiled

Oh, so we've hit our forties now,
and everything is slowing down,
this middle age that I've found
is just dragging me around

Where is that spark I had for a while?

Where is the sparkle,
where is the wonder—
the days when we used to
play in the thunder

splashing through puddles
with rain on my face,
never worrying about how
to put food on my plate

Life is truly an adventure, isn't it?

Choices and paths
we pick and we choose;
none of us truly
know what to do

And yet,
they're still scoring
our credit
just to prove
to the world
we're worth it

It's a curious place,
a curious life

I think we should all
go play outside

We're All Mad Here

Comfort in the Chaos

I find comfort in the chaos
that lingers in my head.
I'm not sure I would feel comfortable
if the chaos was no longer there.

I find my solace in my thoughts
as I weave tales of woe.
Only the grimmest words will do
for the story to unfold.

Witchy women joining together
to battle the monsters
and evil villains,

saving all of the helpless children,
feeding the hungry, and
nurturing the sick and innocent.

And just when it feels
like a gentle hug
wrapping around you
snug as a rug,

the storm blows in
and whips your hair in tangles,
and you're now fighting
with your demons.

The storms I brew
within my fables
are crafted by a
mind in shambles.

Nothing makes sense
until it's out on the pages,
spilled from the ink,
from my fingers.

Yes, I find comfort
inside my mad mind—
a chaotic dungeon
where I find

all of the strangest,
most peculiar creatures
searching for a place
of belonging.

All I do is give them a name;
I write their stories
and play their games;

for if I refuse,
then I will lose
the madness inside
that keeps me sane.

A Witch's Nursery Rhyme

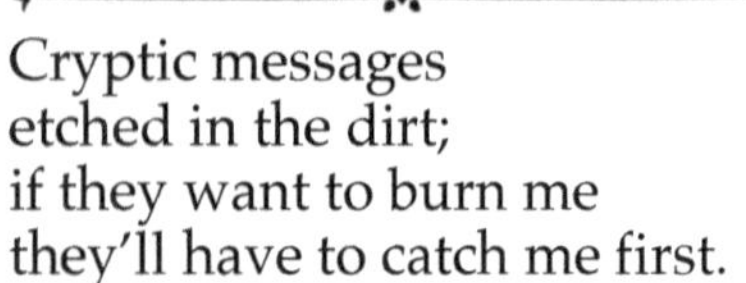

Cryptic messages
etched in the dirt;
if they want to burn me
they'll have to catch me first.

Ring around the fire pole,
they won't stop
till they burn my soul.

They say they're saving me
from sin,
but it's my wicked heart
that will win again.

The evil in their dark
cold hearts
will soon be buried
in the dirt.

Jack will tumble
as Jill stands tall;
Humpty Dumpty
deserved to fall.

All the egos
sitting high in their towers
will soon know what it means
to cower.

We shall not put them
together again;
we will build anew
and the knights won't win.

The witches will rise—
all women and girls—
the ones labeled as man-haters—
will soon rule their world.

It is no longer
a world for man;
they will grovel at our feet
when we're done with them.

We are writing new stories—
not of princesses and peas,
but of strong, witchy women
who don't need to please

any man, or boss, or foe;
we are sick and tired
of doing what we're told.

Gather your pens, your books,
your herbs, and brews;
it is time to craft
something new.

A world where all women
and girls are safe,
where men learn how
to stay in their place.

For if they don't,
we know what to do.
The wicked witches
don't eat children in stew.

We save the largest cauldron
for the most evil-filled men.
We won't rest until
our stomachs are full again.

Love is Never Enough

Sometimes love
just isn't enough.

I love the moon
though I betray her every day
by basking under the sun.

I love a cloudy, rainy day,
though I find joy when
the sunlight is on display.

I have loved too hard
then been let down
by people who would rather
see me drown.

And I am still judged if I
don't sacrifice myself
in the name of love.

Most times, love
just isn't enough.

We all love so many things,
though the world still expects us
to fall in love
with a human who will
likely forget our worth
one day in the future
and we won't feel like enough.

They claim the single women
must be sad, lonely hags
with no purpose in life
other than rescuing cats.
Though, that is a love
far greater than most
as we save innocent creatures
who need a safe home.

Our love is not measured
by a romantic relationship;
our love knows far greater
than a spouse who will berate us
when we do not own up to
the expectations they have bound us to.

No, we love on our own will,
giving it freely to others who feel
that they were forgotten
by a world gone mad—
a world that believes
we must be utterly sad
if we do not find a partner,
if we do not find love from another.

Instead, we spread the love around
to friends and animals we have found,
giving them a safe space to be
who they truly are with no boundaries.

How many parents and partners can say the same?

Yes, love fuels us, but it is more than love.
It is an understanding that love
is never enough.
We must also be willing
to lift each other up,
to let others rise…
just like the moon does
when she lets the sun shine.

Of the Universe

Trace my scars
and discover constellations;
made from the stars,
I am perfection

The stories of my soul
marked on my skin;
the secrets I hold
inked deeper within

At my core,
I am the sun—
a ball of fire
as I burn

The stars reside
inside my bones;
I try to hide
my universe

Planets align
within my head,
a chaotic mind
in constant orbit

The moon, my light,
shines from my eyes,
I take flight
as gravity decides

where I rest,
grounded for now
inside my nest
where I only allow

the kindest souls,
the wildest hearts,
fully whole,
straight from the stars

A Prayer to Hekate

With these words
I call to thee,
Hekate,
place the burden
of fear and pain
away from the women
and toward the men to blame
for all of the hate,
the abuses, the crimes,
the violence and anger
shown to innocent lives;
please let them feel
even an ounce of that hurt;
bless them with
the weight of this curse.
Show them what
it means to be
stripped of their jewels—
their prized dignity.
Oh, Hekate, I only ask of you
to return to sender—
a karma of poetic justice,
hauntingly
ever
after.

Misfits

Feeling like I didn't belong
when I was only six years old,
played along the best I could
tried my hardest to be good.

Though it could not be contained—
the quirky, weirdo personality
and of course, all of the rage.

Decorate my body
like a Christmas tree,
adorned with ornaments
and stars all over me.

I have no style
because I love all of them,
and my weirdo mind
feels awkward quite often.

I get in my pajamas
all snug and comfy
and spend my nights writing
poetry to my kitties.

And just like that I'm strolling
through a graveyard alone,
at peace with the departed
now resting their bones.

No issues at all
watching true crime
while crying endlessly
when an animal dies.

No, I do not fit in anywhere
and that is how I like it,
only connecting with the
other weirdo misfits.

We are all a little strange
with our weirdo tattoos
and our weirdo brains.

I feel my most authentic
weirdo self around
the other weirdos
that I have found.

With our silly little messages
and chats I hold so dear,
in my lovely band of misfits
we're all a little weird here.

Eyes of Approval

I spent too much of my life
seeking others' approval—
their praise, admiration,
affirmation, and delusion
that they determine
what my worth is,
a price tag given
to me at birth.

I truly thought
that their acceptance
meant I belonged,
that I would be successful.
Their stamp of validation
was all I craved—
not realizing I could
pave my own way.

And so, when I discovered
my own voice,
they placed other labels
to mark my worth—
calling me all
the names in the book,
like bitchy, wild, and feral,
as they discovered they
could no longer tame me.

You may think it's a blessing
to be adored,
but at what cost
to little girls?
We are no longer
teaching obedience.
Instead, we are leading
the resistance.

I now prefer to watch
men grovel,
as they claim feminism
is turning us awful.
It is far past time we
should be heard,
should be believed.

And one day, us women will rule,
once we all recognize
that life is not measured by
how we are viewed in others' eyes.

Talk Back Girl

They say back-talker like it's a bad thing…

They call her bossy
and try to tone her down,
attempt to make her feel small
and quiet her mouth.
They have called her all
of the names in the book—
feisty, sassy, bitchy,
loud, rude, obscure.
They refuse to give her
the titles she has earned.

They think they can knock
her crown from her head;
though, she has picked herself up
from the floors where she's bled.
She continues to stand
when they'd love to see her fall.
She continues to shout
and say whatever she wants.
They really hate
to hear her talk.

So, talk back, girl,
give them a show;
all they want
is you in their control.
Never stay quiet,
never bow down.
Talk back, girl,
watch them drown.
Talk-back girls
turn into strong women,
and we need more
in this resistance.
Your words may lead others
to fight back on our side.
So, talk back, girl,
we will not hide.

We will talk back,
we will demand respect;
they will honor our boundaries…
or we'll leave them for dead.
We will not be silenced
by their vicious crimes.
We will talk back
and expose their lies.

Talk-back girls hold power,
that is why they fear us.
Do not lose your talk-back, girl,
it is what makes them powerless.
Speak out, talk back, never shut up.
Your words matter,
so, talk back, girl.

Scars that Linger

I've spent much time
filling in the gaps
of holes left behind
from too much sadness.

Like paper when
it gets wet, shriveled up,
I cannot iron out
all of the wrinkles.

The madness I keep
is buried deep inside of me,
from time to time
skimming the surface.

And I fidget
with it
a little bit
like a scar
that lingers
on my skin—

a beauty mark
that has been embedded
into my soul
to carry with me
wherever I go.

In due time,
they will be patched up,
bandages adorning
my wounds,
stitches weaved
through.

And as I heal,
I still feel
those lacerations,
once too deep,
puncturing me.

Our cuts never seem
to fully disappear,
and so, we must
keep mending
the damage done
from those we loved
as we guide
our own healing.

The Dragon is You

We were taught to fear the dragons,
told they must be slayed
before we can be saved.

Though,
I breathe fire.
I am fueled by rage.
I am starving for peace.

They want us to believe
our anger is unjustified,
our noncompliance unjust.

Nasty women, we are.
Crazy cat ladies.
Witches.
Feral.

Maybe we *have* all gone mad here.

I do not fear the dragons—
innocent creatures they tried to villify.

I wake up from my nightmarish slumber
ready to fight,
baring my teeth,
fire hot on my breath.

I break through the chains that bind me,
rusted from years of being shackled.
I no longer take orders from madmen.
I no longer am bound by their
expectations, their rules, their
governance.

I do not fear the dragon.
I welcome her.

A Bad Witch

Always waiting
for the fucking shoe
to drop and break,
like, fuck you too!

Barely hanging
by a thread,
one thing goes wrong
and I may be dead.

Dodging bullets,
dodging men,
dodging calls—
I'm not talking to them.

Paid the bills—
it's the bare minimum;
fuck student loans,
no one should have to pay them.

And all this time
the world is swallowing me
into a pool, slowly
drowning me.

And I can't fucking breathe.

I'm not letting them
take this from me.

My soul chose this life—
that's the part I forgot;
I often lose sight
that I got what I want.

Proving I'm a Gladiator
every single day,
jumping over all the obstacles
that keep getting in my way.

I am the acrobat
flying high in the sky,
flipping through the air,
reaching new heights.

I am the champion
each day I awake,
proving I'll never
go down without a fight.

And though, I do fear drowning,
I am the swimmer
that moves effortlessly,
weightlessly, through the water.

Even in my middle age,
I am still a bad bitch—
a bad ass woman
who never quits.

Cheshire Smile

It is quite strange, yes,
when a man tells you to smile?
Like we have no idea
what to do with our own mouths
when they walk by?

And they always seem
to expect us to
laugh at their jokes
and pretend they're cute.

It seems quite odd
that they don't understand
that we have our own brains
we use to think for ourselves.

I'm certain they believe
they're doing us a favor—
reminding us how to feel,
how to walk, how to labor.

It is utterly creepy, for sure,
men displaying attraction
to little girls,
and yet, it is *us* who needs reminded
that we still must smile at them.

So, ladies, be sure not to forget
to put a little red sugar on your lips,
pour some red liquid behind your teeth,
and when he tells you to smile,
just grin
and then…

remind him feral women don't owe him shit.

Season of the Witch

It is that time of year again—
a time for meeting up with wicked friends,
as we all gather and begin
to work our spells and poison evil men.

They will say we live in sin,
but I assure you, it is them
who do not follow the rules given
to them inside their sacred bible.

These people are far too judgy for me,
I cannot even believe
that their god loves unconditionally—
but with conditions; it's mad, you see?

I chose to follow this other path,
where witches cackle and go a bit mad
when the full moon is on display;
just like werewolves, we come out to play.

We hunt down the predators
that should have been our saviors;
it was evil men who gave us
the reasons for our wicked behavior.

It is my favorite time of year—
the time that all toxic men should fear—
when the witches are on their hunt,
a season we yearn all year for.

Oh, who am I kidding,
it's not really a season;
we are witches daily,
and only sometimes vicious.

Cackle, Crackle, Curse

I'm love and light,
with a soul as black as night.

If you come in disturbing my peace,
I will not react peacefully.

Respect is earned,
not bargained for.

As I live,
I shall cackle.

And when needed,
the fire shall crackle.

And the fun begins
when I throw them in
and they begin to scream.

We do not live,
laugh, love;

we cackle, crackle,
and ensure they are
cursed for eternity.

Something Wicked this Way Comes

Let me sum it up for you,
the wicked carnival
I'm inviting you to.

It is an experience only for
dreams of little
girls and boys.

A magical place in the woods,
where secrets are kept
from the world.

Where pigs can fly, and you can, too;
there are no limits
restraining you.

The witches are still wicked,
but only toward evil men,

as they dunk them inside
of the alligator
water pit.

Men are trapped in cages, as the tigers stalk outside,
salivating over dinner,
anticipating their next bite.

It is always men dressed up as clowns—
they look like that in real life—
as they drop all the balls they're juggling around.

Red noses,
red shoes,
red hats—
a forehead sticker that says,
"I'm the biggest clown alive."
I swear, it's in the fine print.

I do hope you will join us
on our grand opening day!

It will be such a sight to see—
when men don't get their way.

Let's play…

A Love Spell

She traveled through the woods at night,
a woman—alone—looking for a fight.
Each full moon, without hesitation,
she lured the men full of temptation
into her trap by the water's edge—
a distressed damsel on the ledge.
Her beauty stuns every impure heart—
dangerous men lurking in the dark.
A maiden, so fair, shouldn't be out so late,
he offers to walk her to her gate.
She smiles politely—they like to feel needed—
and takes his hand as he's leading
the gorgeous damsel to a dark fate…
he has no idea that his own death awaits.
For she knows these woods far better than he;
she is of the earth, her home in the trees.
And as he thinks he has the upper hand,
the witch comes out with the wind.
A karmic curse—a simple spell—
return to sender—an eternal hell.

The Wicked Witch of Your Dreams

I'll sneak into your dreams
without a peep,
the puppeteer of your thoughts
as you sleep.
You cannot escape
my prying fingers,
strumming out warnings
while you're dreaming.

I can stir up emotions
you won't have the words for,
cause quite a commotion
you'll pay the price for.

You will beg to wake
from the nightmare before you,
pleading with the witch
behind the curtain.

Though, this isn't Oz
and witches are real.
So, sleep tight, little man;
you'll soon know how we feel.

Capitalism's Victims

Let this be your reminder…

They have no problem replacing you.

They have no problem supporting
others who aren't you.

So do not give them all your energy,
all your power,
all your expertise.

Clock in.
Do your job.
Then get on with your life.

Do not let their capitalism eat you alive.

They claim to love all the people
who contribute to their vision,
and then reward us all with
a gift card for a cup of coffee.

Or better yet, some boxed up pizza.

They want you to make
your job your life.

But don't forget,
you'll never get out alive.

Please, keep some spark for yourself.

And take the time you've earned to rest.

We will never get
our paid time back.
They think we owe them
for paying our check.

That is what this
system teaches,
though they feed off us
just like leeches.

Our labor
pays *their* bills,
and they will never
get their fill.

They've tainted our water
and poisoned our minds
to follow their lead
as we lose our time.

How do we get our excitement back?

It often feels like we have to fake it
until we can make it.

And I just don't have the time for that.

I always do my job well;
I've earned my keep,
and so I can tell
you that it is okay
to want to succeed,
but please do not
let them be the reason
that you bleed.

Not one of us
signed up for this;
we had different dreams
when we were kids.

Do not let this system
steal your magic.
If greed shall win,
it would be most tragic.

You do not have to
climb corporate ladders
for you to know
your life matters.

Where Weirdness Lies

Over Unicorn Mountain,
around Mermaid Bend,
you will find the witches
living in sin.

The walkway there
is paved in bones
from all of the men who
trespassed on their homes.

Their curtains are hung
up in their windows,
sewn from the souls
taken by the widows.

Their well is filled
with toxic men's tears,
used to brew potions
of evil most severe.

Their wicked cackles
fill up the night,
as they dine under the moon
and give men fright.

Though, the rumors of them
have spread far and wide,
luring more men in
without an invite.

The witches only
want their peace,
within their weird space,
living their weird dreams.

A potion here,
a spell there,
a dabble of curse
for the men who deserve

to lose their sanity
and become a bit madder,
as the witches dance
and chant a bit louder.

Until men choose
to leave women alone,
we shall live as witches
amongst our weird coven.

And when they try to
take us by surprise,
we will bury them in the garden
where our weirdness lies.

Playing with Dolls

I comb their hair so gently
so as not to pull or tug.
I snap up the buttons
on their collared shirts;
slip their loafers
on to their feet,
and leave them no weapons
to use on the street.
As they step out
into the world,
surrounded by all manner
of women and girls,
they are graded by
how well they respect
all of the boundaries
given to them.

Once all of the scores
have come in and been tallied,
it is time for a new lesson
in weak, fucking cowards—
the ones who don't listen
when a woman says "no",
the ones who believe
they can take what they want.
But in this dollhouse,
the women rule all;
and vile, toxic men
become my voodoo dolls.

Steven here is guilty
of grabbing a woman's arm
when she tried to walk by,
only wanting to be left alone.
And Kyle has proven
he is too weak
to lead a lady
or allow her to think.

Bobby is convicted
of horrors most foul,
as he strips women bare
of all of their power.
Timothy is accused
of preying eyes
and not respecting privacy
in women's lives.
And, oh, there are more
men who don't see—
simply because he's a *nice* guy,
he *must* be believed.
And the men who don't care
to respect women's boundaries,
sneaking up, stalking,
and hiding like cowards.

No, in this dollhouse, they will
come out into the light
where it is the women who will
give them a fright.
And with much delight,
I will lead each of the dolls
where the cauldron is flaming
and burning hot.
As the women chant,
and sing, and spell,
one by one, the dolls
will tell
all of their secrets,
their scandals, their lies,
all their abuses,
their tortures, their crimes.
And each conviction
will feel so sweet,
as they are dropped into
the cauldron by their feet.
This planet will be better
once we are done
cleaning up the earth
of all of its scum,
and making more space
for beauty to bloom.

We will build a world
where there is no room
for men's evil ways,
for their control and greed.
This is the dollhouse
of every woman's dreams.

A Haunted Mind

Inside this haunted house
within my haunted mind,
I'm cleaning out the cobwebs
of a past I left behind.

You can always start a new life.

The floorboards may be creaky,
dust has settled on the beams,
and skeletons are definitely lurking,
haunting all my dreams.

There are ghosts hiding
in the dark corners of the attic;
sometimes it's quite difficult
to find the right balance

between enjoying the peace
and wanting to scream.

I'm afraid I'll never fight off these demons inside of me.

But I can sweep…

A little cleaning never hurt;
scrub the windows of all the dirt,
so I can let a bit more light inside;
no need to retreat or to hide
inside this haunted house
within my haunted mind.

I can make friends with ghouls
and hungry vampires,
tame the dragons
that once conspired

with my enemies
to take me down.
I can unbury the secrets
inside this house.

My walls may remain
a bit dark and macabre
with strange and mysterious
trinkets in my shadow box,

though I can dance
with all the beasts
haunting my mind
and tormenting me.

I've always loved a festive party.

Oh, the doors are opening
then slamming shut,
my thoughts flung about as I
clamber and try to pick them up.

Bobbing for apples,
but all I catch are teeth
falling out
inside my dreams.

Freddy is there just laughing at me.

Oh, sure, I could just
pack up and leave
behind all the boxes
stacked inside my memory.

But they would never let me be,
forever and always haunting me.

And so, I simply must clean
and prepare for a never-ending Halloween
inside this haunted mind
in this haunted house where I reside.

The Very Hungry Witch

The little old witch
who lived in the woods
set out every day
to search for food.
She gathered mushrooms,
she gathered berries,
as she chatted with
all the faeries.
Though, on this day
the resources were few,
as winter approached;
she wasn't sure what to do.
The apples were rotting,
the squirrels hid all the nuts;
and the little old witch
was left without much.

The faeries were her
mischievous friends,
and they fed her ideas
for hunting down men.
They promised her meat
most tasty,
though their blood was black
and must be wasted.

And so she set off on a new path,
to hunt down vicious predators.
She would wait until night, as she
wasn't afraid of the dark dangers.
She rarely ate meat—
she loved all earth's creatures—
but she was most certain
the evil men had it coming.
And her stomach was rumbling.

As she stumbled upon the hunters
killing the defenseless deer in numbers,
she did not even hesitate
to take off their heads for her plate.

She kept on her voyage,
taking different routes,
considering what kind of sauce
she'd want on her palate.
She never cared much
for spicy foods,
but vicious men
might taste quite good.

And as she hunted her own predators down,
she saved many creatures from their fate.
And she filled up her freezer for winter,
with plenty meals for her to eat.

A Witch's Mind

When it is warm and sunny
my brain is too foggy
to pull out the macabre
to pull out the creepy

Melting away on a summer day
does not drive my creativity
so I find myself writing late
beneath the moon to light me

I may pull a dark thought
here and there
but it takes more effort
to craft words of fear

Though as that first
Fall breeze comes through
my dark mind awakens
from her summer gloom

She lights the cauldron
throws in some words
dreams darker dreams
and weaves a new curse

She doesn't lure children
into her oven
she prefers sacrificing men
along with her coven

She loves to think up
grisly, dark stories
of eating the rich
of tales most gory

The cauldron brewing
and boiling over
as she concocts
a spellbook story

Ghoulish monsters
and beasts with fangs
evil villains
and feminist rage

The witch that lives inside my mind
is eager for the call
as my thoughts grow
darker in the fall

Feed the Beast.

My body splayed
                a canvas

His eyes of lust
                and venom

I begged…
                have mercy!

And then
                he devoured me

Cleopatra's Power

Somewhere in Egypt
the last pharaoh is buried
in a hidden tomb
as her legacy is carried
across centuries
and generations—
the final leader
of her kingdom.

Cleopatra refused to bow
to any man or king,
devoting her life
to protect her people
from the hands
and the rising power
of the empire of Rome.

At the end,
she lost her fight,
but did so in
her own way.
A woman wise
beyond her years,
knowing men's
vicious games.

And Cleopatra
ended her life
in whatever way
she knew how.
She refused
to allow
any man
to claim her.
That is her legacy,
her gift to women—
that is Cleopatra's power.

A Haunted Carriage Ride

At the stroke of midnight,
the pumpkin does not vanish.
Instead, it turns into
a truly haunted carriage.

If you insist on taking a ride,
you may be quite surprised
that the carriage will give you a fright,
leaving children screaming with much delight.

The only price that you must pay
is a small drop of your blood;
there is no time to delay,
so please, do make a cut.

As the jack-o'-lantern transforms,
a skeleton horse appears
to pull the carriage into the night
where awaits your fears.

So, hop on in; do not fret,
this is as haunted as it gets.
The werewolves wait inside the trees
as a chill sits on the breeze.

And overhead, the bats do fly
as they get ready to haunt the night
as the carriage passes by…
there are no refunds for this ride.

There is no need for the vampires
to ask permission to enter,
for they have already been invited
to feed on you for dinner.

And the wicked witches
are waiting just beyond the trees
to place a curse onto your bones,
bringing you to your knees.

All the black cats that cross your path
are slowly stealing your soul,
as they laugh and drag you back
into the witches' home.

The cauldron is hanging over the flame,
waiting for ingredients to be tossed in.
There is really no time to delay,
as the delivery must begin.

You will not remember a thing I've said,
as the vampires wipe your memory.
It is now time to climb inside
of this haunted carriage ride,
as the pot awaits for simmering.

Wish Granted

My heart is so damn heavy.
While it may be because of him,
it's heavy for the people
who are affected
by the evil this country elected.

Celebrating with Nazi salutes,
acting like they can do
whatever the fuck they want to.

I do not take hate lightly;
there are few things I loathe,
but leaving desperate people
to figure it out on their own—
out in the cold…
all they fucking have is their hope.

No law or rule book will change
someone's identity or strip away
the resilience that the oppressed
have finally gained.

Their words and actions and laws
will only fuel our cause,
steer us forward without pause.

It does get exhausting and wearisome
carrying around a heart that is burdened,
but I have lifted heavier stones,
that is for certain.

And together, this war will be waged;
they cannot dismantle all of this rage.
We will burn the fucking cage
if they think they will stop us.

They want evil?
They want hate?
I cannot fucking wait.
I'll be the first to celebrate
when we tear down the gates
and watch them take
their very last
evil
breaths.

Blow out the candles
on the cake.

Wish granted.

Retribution

I have deemed myself,
on this darkest night,
judge, jury, executioner,
here to end this fight.

The battle has been waging
for years and years,
and women are now raging,
no longer in fear.

The Devil has chosen a side now
and She is here to stay,
ruler of the underworld
digging all the graves.

The witches are gathering
underneath the full moon,
lighting the fire for the sacrifice
that is coming soon.

A chant for protection
of all of the innocent,
a chant for freedom
following their vengeance.

As they gather—
thousands deep—
they chant for hope,
they chant for peace.

Though their spells
cannot come to light
if they do not march,
if they do not fight.

The potions brewed
will go to waste,
so they cannot falter;
they must move in haste.

The witches know
it is their fate—
they will be burned
at the stake

if they do not find
a solution,
so they must get
their retribution.

Monster Ball

You are cordially invited to the Ball of the year,
a fantastic display of all we should fear.

Monsters in alleys, prowling on women,
cat-calling and terrorizing,
telling them to grin.

And as the monsters dance their dance,
the lowly women reach out their hands
to be twirled right in place,
as the monsters bow with ghastly grace.

But the excitement does not end there;
it is only the beginning
when the villain is dancing.

And I just can't wait to show you all
the work I've put into this Ball.

Oh, ladies, please adorn your masks,
as we do not need any witnesses
to this monstrous celebration—
a Ball truly for the ages.

Don't forget to bring a plus one!
The more the merrier,
and more the fun.

She is the Darkness

They lure us out, like we're prey,
as if they have already dug our graves.

It is now *our* turn to fight back and make them learn women are
not their victims.

We are their monsters.

We are now *their* predators.

And when the predator becomes the prey,
they underestimate our rage.

Believing us to be weak,
as we hunt them down on the street.

Hide in gutters and watch them scream,
as we pull our knives from our dress—with pockets.

We'll be the nightmare they'll never forget.

And the one they'll wish
they *were* nice to.

Treat us better…
or end up dead.

We're All Mad Here

Spewing and splashing, swinging and slashing; I just may cut off somebody's head!

Bring me my wine, so that I may dine while my enemies are buried nearby.

I do not have time to be judge and jury, and so I will execute with all of my fury—an ending full of torture and cruelty.

Devour my words, taste them as they land, and know that they are just the beginning.

I do intend to defend my space—and my peace—from volatile men.

I do not meddle in trash; I will take out the garbage…just after I have cleaned up all of the filth and carnage.

And so, if you think I am all talk—all words—that I do not have the heart—the guts—to shut men up, I dare you to consider—

in this wonderland, we are all mad here; and, oh, also, please remember,

when the rabbit is late, for our dinner date, I'll be glad to add you to the menu.

Off With Their Heads!

Off With Their Heads

I've had enough,
I'm sick of this;
children dying,
no meds for the sick.
The rich are laughing
and demanding more,
as we are begging and screaming
to help the poor.
I played my cards right
time and again,
laid out all my aces,
trying to win.
But they hoarded the cards,
hidden out of sight,
laid down their flush
with such delight.
They say they earned it—
they won fair and square,
but this game isn't equal
and no one will dare
to stop them from
their cheats and lies,
as we go all-in
on a pair of fives.
The dealer is not
shuffling,
but giving the same wins
back to them.
It does not matter
that we know;
they'll deny and defend
until we depose
all of the evil
from all of the seats;
scrub out the filth
and have our defeat.
They'll keep throwing
their money out on the table,
scooping ours up
as if we should pay them.

But I'm stacking my deck,
preparing a new game,
where all other cards
defeat King and Queen.
I refuse to fold,
as they hope we all do;
I have more up my sleeve—
a trick or two.
I no longer play nice
with spades, clubs,
diamonds, and hearts;
I have the swords stacked
in my tarot cards.
My ten of swords is calling for
the end—a resolution—
to this nightmare we're all facing,
and I've found a solution.
It is time for them to learn
the rules of *our* game,
time for them to fold,
time for them to pay.
We'll pull from the cards,
swords and daggers,
read them their fortune,
laugh as they stagger.
For in this deck
it is stacked with dread;
pull out a card,
off with their heads!

Long Live the Queen!

They want us scared—
don't fall for it!
Their only plan
is intimidation.
Do not forget
we outnumber them
when we join together,
when we hold hands.

Stop giving in to their
demands!

Instead, I suggest,
something more fun—
go outside and play
and run.

Kick a ball around
with your kids.
Stop listening to
their bullshit.

Don't give them
the reaction they want;
enjoy your loved ones
and protect the flock.

Find joy in the flowers
and the leaves turning
colors.
Love yourself harder
and love one another.

They so desperately want
hate to win.
They don't know what it
means
to have loving friends.

The kindest souls
are *not* the weakest.
Their mistake is thinking
they can defeat us.

Don't forget,
in every fairytale story
that we've read,

the villain shows
their evil face
to control all people
within their space.

And as the story
continues on,
there are more heroes
standing strong.

As the people grow
in countless numbers,
it becomes quite easy
to take down the soldiers.

So, stop listening to
all of the dread
that they want filling
up our heads.

They can yap
and spew their hate,
but if no one listens
they'll one day break.

And then we can
walk right in
and take back *our* house
they're living in.

We do not need
to move in haste;
it is far better
to make them wait

and wonder what
we're all up to.
And they will find
our joy in bloom,

leaving them all quite
confused.

Find your balance
for staying informed,
but not overwhelmed
by all their reports.

Their entire plan
is utter confusion,
so let's play their game
right back at them.

Help your neighbors
who need a bit more.
Pick others up
off of the floor.

Laugh with your children
and with your friends,
and keep on
reminding them

that we are all capable of
taking down the tyrant
with all of the others
standing beside us.

We will know
when the time is right
to gather together
and to fight

amongst our enemies—
not amongst one another.
Please, don't forget
all of our poor sisters and
brothers.

And we will one day
gloriously reign,
and women *will*
lead the way.

It might feel
a bit impossible,
as we're buried in
patriarchal capital.

But I promise you
if we fight and *believe,*
we will *finally*
have a Queen.

And long may she live—
all of the women,
ruling our land,
and caring for *all* the
children.

The Lion's Den

Anger is our friend,
complacency the enemy.
We will not bow down
to any male toxicity.

They need their guns
to feel big and strong.
But all the witches need
is a spell and a song.

Though, it's still fun
to bring along our swords,
and string our bows and arrows
to pierce their evil hearts.

We shall allow them
to start the fire
that we will throw them in
as this war transpires.

We can make them think
we are mighty weak—
just poor damsels
they need to keep

under their wing,
within their homes—
in the lion's den
where we know

they must fall asleep
at night,
and then we will give them
quite a fright.

No more weak women;
we don't need a white knight.
We will become the bears,
and we will win this fight.

Shopping Trip

He said he loved her,
he promised it so;
she vowed to be loyal,
to let their love grow.

The honeymoon phase
was utter, pure bliss.
She had never had anyone
love her like this.

She would not look elsewhere,
this love was so true;
she kept all of her promises,
even the tiny ones, too.

She promised to love him,
to hold all his secrets;
she promised to trust him,
and she really meant it.

That fairytale story
is all she hoped for;
oh, how lucky she was
to find a man who chose her.

Then late one night,
on a stormy eve,
a raven approached
her window with the breeze.

The slightest tapping
startled her so,
for she felt uneasy
when he wasn't home.

But the raven was
a friend to her,
she opened the window
and in flew the bird.

A message it carried
and delivered to her hand,
detailing his treachery
known by all of the land.

His secrets were protected
by friends, family, neighbors;
they concealed his truth
while she did all the labor.

For man should have
the freedom to
do as he pleases,
make his own rules.

But his bride did not follow
the law of man,
she wrote her own edicts,
controlled her own hands.

As she thanked the raven,
she wiped a single tear from her eye,
slipped on her cloak,
and walked into the night.

She had her own coin,
she never needed his,
and it was time for
a shopping trip.

She knocked on the door
knowing the business was closed,
but when the door opened,
she was guided into the funeral home.

"How much for this box?"
she asked without grief;
her back had been stabbed,
her trust had been thieved.

She thanked the old lady
for allowing her to stop in,
and go shoppin' for his coffin
he'd soon be buried in.

Baby, It's Dark Outside

I really should leave
    Baby, it's dark outside
I can take care of me
    The monsters are wild at night
I really can't dwell
    I can walk you, still
I'll be just fine
    It's the darkest night

There really is no need to worry
    I truly think you need me to walk you
I'll be home in a hurry
    Maybe you should stay a bit longer
I promise, I know these streets well
    Having a chauffeur would really help
I really have nothing to fear
    You have no idea what awaits out there

There is no need for you to join me
    I can get you home in a hurry
Fine, if you really insist to escort me
    And maybe then I can stay over?
That is not a part of the plan
    Baby, let me just be the man
I guess you better grab your jacket
    Now, that's more like it

Come on, this way
    What is that up ahead?
It's a quicker way
    It looks like a dead end
There's no need to fret
    It's completely filling me with dread
It's just the witches' dance
    Wait is that blood on the ground?
Now let me lead you to your death

When a man doesn't listen
    I promise I meant nothing vicious
And insists on joining in on my missions
    I didn't mean to make you suspicious
Now, baby, that's quite alright
    I should just turn back now
But it's time for the sacrifice…
    Oh, shit, I didn't mean it!

Baby, when it's
dark
outside

Speak No Evil, Do No Harm

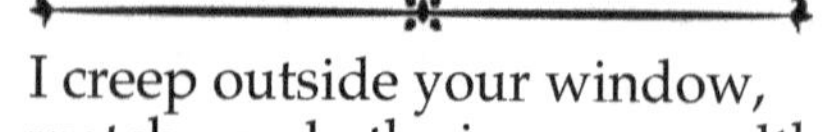

I creep outside your window,
watch you bathe in your wealth,
as all of the people outside
suffer and starve to death.

I am no Robin Hood
here to steal your gold,
but the villain you made me
when you kicked us out in the cold.

I watch your every movement
as you polish your jewelry,
take note of your predictable routine,
as I am in no hurry.

I will capture your betrayals,
record your every indiscretion,
laugh when you are startled
as you look out in suspicion.

Though you will not see me,
as my crows cause a commotion,
and I slip inside
find a place to hide—
this mission my devotion.

For the people are starving,
children getting sicker;
they need a protector,
not a false tyrant king dictator.

I'll be the villain in your story,
the witch with a wicked scheme,
as I set my targets on your bones;
I can show you what cruelty means.

I place my unending empathy
closed up inside my locket;
for I won't be needing it here
in this tower you're sheltered in.

It is time for your walls to crumble,
time for your castle to burn;
for men who perpetrate evil
shall earn all the harm.

Huntress

Through the night, I trek,
I do not fear or fret;
within the trees I move
beneath the wicked moon.

I take my time
to get it right,
set my traps
to trick the lads.

It must finally end—
them hunting down
my animal friends.

Women have reclaimed
these woods again.

I stash my arrows
upon my back,
find a tree to climb.

I wait patiently
with my snacks
and the birds up high.

I have plenty of time.

As branches snap
beneath the tree,
I look down
and I see

a man taking aim
with his rifle,
and I have to
quickly stifle

the gasp I feel
within my chest,
afraid I'll be too late,
and another animal dead.

I steady my bow
upon my shoulder,
set my sights
on my target,

release the string
just in time,
as his finger
reaches the trigger.

I never miss,
I've trained well.

The woods belong
to women;
we make
the rules now.

It is Time...

We have heard the stories
and watched the torture.
We have marched in peace.

Now, it's time for torches.

They have stripped our rights,
and stolen our coins.
Still, they claim, it's all
in the name of their lord.

They use their bibles
while they spew their hate.
They want us terrified
to be hung on the stake.

They are betting on our demise,
as they kidnap people,
as children and women die.

Their plan is chaos
until we admit defeat.
They won't be satisfied
until we grovel at their feet.

Though, they have underestimated
the power of women—of witches—
when we join together.

It is time to take back our peace.
It is time to let them see
that there is more power
in our veins,
running through our bones,
releasing from our hands.

They do not believe that we
are bound to the stars,
holding the moon's energy
within our arms.

They may bring their
guns and bombs,
but we dance in nature
with the Mother Universe.

And no one—nothing—
is more powerful
than a mother—a woman—
protecting her own.

So, gather now, witches,
as we bring together our power.
Raise up your arms
and bury their towers.

Charge up your crystals,
mix your potions and powders.
Light your candles,
chant your spells louder.

Now is not the time to
fight against one another;
it is time to join forces
to help all of the others.

Wear your black tourmaline—
sealed with protection.
Carry clear quartz
to ward off detection.

Meet me at midnight
under the moon.
It is time to show them
what witches can do.

Savage

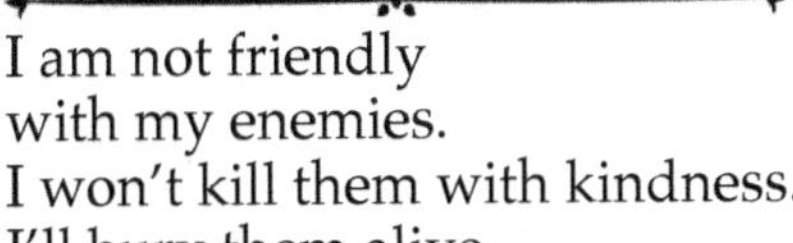

I am not friendly
with my enemies.
I won't kill them with kindness.
I'll bury them alive.

Eyes of daggers,
words of venom,
make them suffer
as they do others.

I protect the meek and innocent,
crafting nightmares their bullies
won't forget.

Watch them bleed
as they cry out, "why?!"
As if they don't see
their toxic shit.

Walk away with grace—
and a bloody knife,
their death engraved
in my memory for life.

Smile sweetly as I go to sleep
knowing they're buried
beneath my feet.

Underground Lair

I slip inside the back door,
tippy-toeing on the floor,
so as not to wake my friend;
I just need to use her basement.

I tried so hard to be good,
but men just never leave me alone,
and so, I must bury them
bones and all in the basement.

Beneath the floor boards, I dig
with a shovel, after I pick
the place where he will be sent
deep in the dirt under the basement.

She and I, we picked her home
as a resting place for their bones.
My friend never charges rent
when I bury the bodies in her basement.

Oh, the time that I have spent
sending men to their deaths.
All my favorite feral women
have bodies buried in the basement.

The Harvest

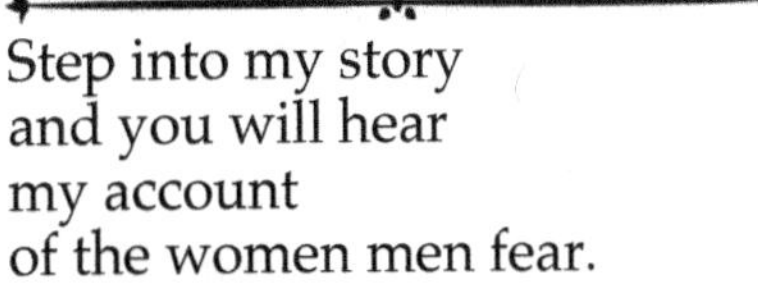

Step into my story
and you will hear
my account
of the women men fear.

Follow me, ladies,
hear my tale
of the men thrown in
to the wishing well,

as the women
wished for abundance
for their crops
for the winter.

The women were
their own farmhands
and the owners
of their own land.

It was their intention
to ensure they receive prosperity
from their wishes.

Coins never seemed to work,
and they couldn't afford
to keep paying more.

And so they plowed
their own fields,
and planted the seeds
and watered them,

threw the men into the well
for their wish to come true—
a harvest they can sell.

Cursed

They call us chicks,
bitches,
females,
witches.
Anything to make us feel
less human.

Just objects for their using.

They love our bodies
but hate our minds;
love our curves,
hate our words.
Love our eyes,
our hips, and thighs,
but want to wreck
our universe.

And so, they must be cursed.

A freezer spell
may not do well,
I think we will need
some fire.
They call us wicked,
so that's what they'll get—
a new spell must be transpired.

We shall knock out their teeth,
strip all the meat
off of their bones
placed in the friend zone
they claim we threw them into.

And in our garden,
we shall bury them—
more fertilizer for the harvest.

If you want to be safe
from the witches' rage,
then be a man who
can be trusted.

For, when men attack,
the witches fight back,
and we always win.
For, we have nine lives
like a cat,
and we cannot be silenced.

And with our words
and magic in our bones,
we chant the curse
that steals men's souls.

And you cannot make a deal with this devil.

Continue calling us what you must,
and we will make sure you're heard,
as you scream from within the fire.

Kill the Beast!

They cheated, they lied,
tried to strip our pride.
They touched and they grabbed
without consent.
They left behind bruises
on our bodies and egos.

And now it is time
to finish them.

They think they are stronger
just because they are broader.
They think we are weak
and just oh, so meek;
they forget we are clever
and oh, so much better
at playing their games
they invented for us.

And now it is time
to cut them up.

As we gather in numbers,
we grow stronger and stronger,
no more weak mothers,
sisters, or daughters.
We all win
when we rise together.

And now it is time
to bury them.

We shall leave no trace
as we clean up the mess;
for the men always disappear—
that's what they do best.
I'm positive no one will find
what we did here tonight.
And so, we shall
invite our guests…

It's time to
kill the beast!

As the Bough Breaks

Sitting in their branches
feeling so tall,
when the bough breaks,
the rich will fall.

And we have come
to cut down the tree
where they are hiding
with their greed.

They killed off the birds
to steal their home,
believing they are safe
from any harm.

They believe their gold
will save them,
while we are down below
doing all the labor.

And so, it is time
for the wind to blow
and rattle their branches
as we chop below.

Watch it crumble,
watch it fall,
as the patriarchy dies
once and for all.

Blood Suckers

The leeches will drain you
of all of your sustenance
when they don't get their way,
retracting their covenants.

Agreements mean nothing
when you make deals with them;
they don't keep promises,
they have no regret.

Like mosquitos
on the hunt,
they seek you out
to drain your blood.

And they take, and take, and take too much.

Just a bunch of blood suckers
I dare to confront.

And so, I will be the vampire bat;
though I don't technically suck, I actually lap,
after sinking in my fangs
to the skin of my prey.

I will keep drinking
until they are drained.

And then I will return
to my dark cave
within the tree hollows
with my colony,

and I will feed
all the bat mothers
who have small infants
and can't hunt with the others.

Unlike other bats,
I can walk, run, and hop
to approach my prey
on my little haunt.

For vampire bats
take care of each other,
unlike the leeches
who drain you of all of your color.

When night falls,
it's time to transition
into my true form
and take my position—

stalking my prey
from up high and down low,
doing the witch's bidding
along with the crow.

A Wicked Hunt

I checked off my tasks,
I ran my errands,
paid my bills, and
cuddled my animals.

I checked the news—
still sad and grim—
children still starving
and men are still men.

It is now time to get some revenge.

Another day is done
and now it's time to
have some fun;
won't you join me
on my wicked hunt?

We prey on the men
with evil souls,
with toxicity in their veins,
and hate in their bones.
We can smell the racism
and the gaslighters,
we can taste the hatred
they have trapped inside them.
We hunt for the rapists
and the pedophiles;
we will track them down
and then we shall defile.
We do not wait for
anyone's permission;
we will be judge, jury, and
executioner to our victims.
We no longer accept
apologies,
we no longer take
losses with grace.
We do not bow to
pedophile kings.

We now bathe
in their screams.
We sacrifice them
to the old gods,
with vengeance
in our hearts.
We shall not give
them a proper burial,
we will burn the leftovers
and let the wind carry them
back into space,
where hate and greed
have no place.

And then we shall dance
around the fire
under the moon
as it guides us.
We will gather together
and celebrate
hunting down
all the hate.

And each day
when night has begun,
we will join again
on our wicked hunt.

The Haunted Characters that I Keep

You fuck with women
because you think we are weak

You didn't know what you were getting
when you chose to fuck with me

Like Freddy, stalking your dreams,
jumping out and making you scream

Like Jason, chasing you through the trees,
I cannot wait to watch you bleed

And like Michael, I keep coming back,
a never-ending story, a never-ending attack

With the chainsaw I rev up,
I laugh and grin as I chop you up

I am Candy (Wo)man in the mirror,
reaching for you when the light flickers

I'll be the shark with the sharpest teeth,
jumping from the waters so that I may feast

Many will think this is all quite evil,
forgetting that men started this little quarrel

All my life, stories have been filled
with cruel men who hunt women and kill

Now it's *our* turn to turn predator;
we will become the evil monsters

Pedophile Tyrant

He purchased the votes
that got him to the top,
didn't even try to hide that
his position had been bought

he claims it's
locker room talk
—forcing women
(and children)
to kiss him
while he gropes them—
and the good ole boys
laugh and encourage him

and then wonder why people loathe him

and they hide the lists
(that don't exist)
as they deny and deny
and defend and defend

mister pedophile tyrant,
we know the truth,
we know about the lies,
we know about the youth
whose innocence died
because of you

we don't need the fucking proof

there in your mansion
and on his island,
you abused little girls
and we know you are lying
about all the women you've raped;
all you know how to do is
take and take
and hate and hate

we will *never* stop talking
about what you've done
without consent
to little girls' bodies

one day (soon)
you'll be gone forever,
and the hate you spewed
buried with you
beneath the ground
we will stomp on;
you deserve no respect
no matter your title

you've torn up
our house—the people's,
ruined *our* garden,
destroyed our safety

you've brought enemies
to our doors,
praising them in hopes
they'll give you
what you want

with absolutely zero concern for the flock

we will carry on
marching against you,
calling out your lies
and manipulated truths

you will never stop us,
you're far too weak,
your bones too brittle,
your heart too meek

your time will be gone in a blink

you don't even respect
your own supporters,
calling them unintelligent;
though, you're all traitors

no, pedophile tyrant,
we don't listen to you;
we laugh and we mock
because it's easy to do

you don't even know
the right words
to use to pretend
you're intelligent

we all know the fucking truth

and one day (soon)
we will celebrate
as your casket is dropped
into your grave

A Lamb in Wolf's Clothing

Gentle as a lamb,
caring for my flock;
a sensitive creature,
I don't pretend to be
what I'm not.

Though, when needed
I put on my cloak,
dressed as a wolf
to protect my own.

I can fight the battles,
endure the pain;
I can find joy in others'
well-deserved gain.

With a heart of gold
(and teeth of daggers)
I can save the innocent
(and masticate the others).

I am but a lamb,
full of hope and love;
but I do not take kindly
to being shoved.

Like a werewolf
under the full moon,
I turn from sheep to monster
so they may pay their dues.

I am not luring
girls in red cloaks;
I'm intimidating men
and making them choke.

I'm not dressing up as a granny,
snug in my bed;
I'm sneaking into men's dreams
and scaring them dead.

I pack up my basket
to head out on my path,
delivering goods to the needy
before I spew my wrath.

I can care for the innocent,
want liberty for all,
and that includes justice
for the evil in the world.

Do not let my kind heart fool you;
I know when to set it aside.
And I'll adorn the cloak of the wolf
as long as evil men are alive.

Wealth of Venom

They spewed their hateful words,
voiced their misguided opinions,
chose what was true in their own eyes
with no concern for the victims.
They want to push my buttons,
they want to watch me burn,
but they don't know that I live in fire
and their words can never hurt.
They will try to manipulate me,
they'll try to break me down;
though, I will cackle and curse
as I rise from the ground.
The venom they spew
is written into my spell,
and now I will be collecting
all of their wealth.
Their hateful words are turned
into gold, stripped from their coins;
as they lose their pensions,
I will take their voice.
When you speak evil, you do harm
to yourself, as you become the target
of a tired old witch
who needs a little practice.
So, allow me just a moment
to fuel the fire for the hearth
that will be used to transmute
your venomous words into my wealth.

Cat Got Your Tongue?

They have backed us into a corner,
stolen our chance for survival.
And all around, we hear the same—
people suffering and dying.

We bought the plan,
we paid our copays,
met deductibles
and signed all the right papers.

We saved the receipts,
we begged and we pleaded,
just give us the medicine
the doctor says we're needing!

I am the Cat Witch,
slipping into the doors
they thought were locked
on restricted floors.

But I am stealthy and
I've been granted nine lives,
and so I will use each of them
to sentence them for their crimes.

They stamp *deny*,
so we must defend;
we gave them the wealth
they are swimming in.

I finally found him—
the big head honcho,
up in his penthouse
enjoying his freedom.

It's easy to trick them
when you act like a damsel
in distress, and they
think they can handle
all of your strength…
because they think we are weak.

I gave him a chance
to defend his own stance;
why has *my* life
been denied—
your pockets stay full
with premiums too high.

And as he called me
"sweetie" and "baby",
mansplaining my plan,
as if more money would save me…

I rolled my eyes at his ignorance,
I took out my knife, and sliced.
It stopped him dead—
as he bled—
when I replied
"Cat got your tongue?
Sorry, but that's not
covered by
your insurance."

A Haunting End

The boy fell in love
with the pretty girl,
he promised to make
her his whole world.
She agreed
to take his hand
bound forever
on this land.
Though, after that day
of their fairytale wedding,
the groom turned into
a gruesome monster.
He showed his fangs,
extracted his claws
without a reason
without a cause.
The girl did not know
what made him so mad,
or why he now treated
her so bad(ly).
She pondered
she wondered
she thought,
then she schemed;
she would not
tolerate
such atrocities.

She stated her boundaries
that he refused to honor,
so she enrolled him
as an organ donor.
And the girl took
her precious time
taking the parts
that could save other lives.
He would no longer need
them
once she was done;
his betrayal of her
made this part extra fun.
She needed a sacrifice
to bring to her coven,
and he sealed his fate,
now locked in the oven.

This story is a
cautionary tale
of a haunting end
for men
who lie, cheat, and steal.

Consensual Prison

These men cry out that they're terrified
that women will accuse them of crimes
if they even go in for a hug
without asking if she's comfortable.

They want the incels to believe
they are entitled to our bodies.
And they cry, oh, woe is me
when we let them down gently.

They designed a hell zone for us to put them in,
when all we said was we want to be friends.
And the entire time they're just lingering,
thinking if they're "nice" we'll change our minds again.

They keep on trying
when we say "No"
and still wonder why
we're happier alone.

They've locked themselves into a box—
a prison of anger for what women want.
They don't even try to understand
what behaviors are acceptable from a man.

They want to be women's leader
but have no idea how to lead.
They want to spread their toxicity
by spreading their seed.

And forcing *us* into this deed.

And this is why we scream.

This male loneliness epidemic
is not women's responsibility to manage.
So, learn our rules and our definitions,
or you *will* find us in our kitchens

pulling out all the knives
to teach you about consent.
Don't fuck with us anymore,
or we'll be the wardens in the prison
you trapped yourself in.

Gravekeeper

They cannot steal my pride.
They cannot steal my sparkle.
They cannot steal my joy.
They cannot steal my cackle.

I will continue to rise
each and every time
this world tries
to knock me down.

I always lift myself off the ground.

And I will laugh right in their face
when they realize they couldn't defeat me.
I don't mind being the villain in their story,
for in my fairytale, I scare them silly.

No, they cannot take
the madness from me;
it's etched in my bones
inside of me,
and even when they
make me bleed,
my power remains
attached to me.

They will regret the day
they ever thought I was weak.

There is nothing that can save
them from their wicked fate,
for I hold the keys to their grave,
and I sure do love to play

in the cemetery, under the moon,
basking in the energy of their doom,
watching the flowers as they bloom
upon the ground outside their tombs.

I will be the keeper of their bones,
their final resting place.
It is a job I hold quite dear,
my winning card, my ace.
Though I love hearts, and
clubs, and diamonds,
I rule with my spade.

Here in my graveyard
where all the traitors are laid.

Let Them Choke

They threaten our safety
when we don't do as they say,
puffing out their chests
when they don't get their way.
Someone somewhere told them
and made them believe
they should try harder
when they don't first succeed.
And no, we aren't talking about
learning a new game,
taking up a new hobby,
or studying a new trade.
They believe they deserve
for us to change our minds
just so they can be pleased
and save their own pride.
They see "no" as utter rejection,
not a simple decision we made
for ourselves, our lives, and now
our livelihood's at stake.

This male loneliness epidemic
is not for women to solve.
We have clearly stated our boundaries
with absolutely no resolve.
We have shouted and screamed,
we have sworn off men,
we have given more chances
again and again.
I'm not sure about you,
but ladies, I'm spent;
I have no more energy
to use on saving them.

My boundaries are not negotiable;
they won't be altered or adjusted
to make some man feel strong,
powerful, or wanted.
I am no longer walking on eggshells
when some man says I can't take a joke.
I no longer have oxygen to spare…
I'll let them fucking choke.

A Very Hungry Monster

I am famished.
I am drained
of all my energy,
no longer sane.
The full moon is rising
and I am feeling weak;
I need to rest,
but I also need to feed.

They wanted to strip me
of all of my power,
thinking they could break me,
but it is them who are cowards.
They have chained me
up inside of this cell
because they are afraid
of the strength I have held
onto all this time.
And they must pay
for all their crimes.

They are unaware of my secret—
that I am fueled and transformed
by the full moon above;
I will soon take my full form.
And it is almost time for them
to join me in my cage,
as they peek in to see me
bottling up all of my rage.

Locked away in here
I have not been given
appropriate meals
or proper nutrition.
They made a mistake believing
hunger makes me weak.
Though, when the full moon arrives,
the monster must feed…

Mean Girls

Here they go, tearing other women down.
Judging their clothes, their eyebrows, their bodies,
forcing a competition
that no one else started.

Inside their mean book
writing their mean words—
men already did this
shit to us first.

And we are not allowing it from some fucking mean girls.

Slip inside
as they sleep,
chop the locks of hair
they wish to keep.

Slip some extra calories
into their food,
let them swell up
like balloons.

Steal their men
right from their grasp,
it's really not so hard
convincing them.

Break their heels
and watch them fall
as they stumble
down the walk.

Change all the numbers
in their phone
so they send their secrets
to the wrong ones.

Place a little Nair
inside their shampoo;
now let's see
who they're mean to.

So, no, I may never
be any thinner,
but fuck the mean girls;
I can be meaner.

Crafting My Castle

I am constructing a palace so great,
it will make evil men meet their well-deserved fate.
I do not want to hesitate
in getting all of these bricks laid.

I am crafting my castle
with secret, locked doors,
and where I can bury bones
beneath the floors.

If men try to enter
without an invitation,
they will be struck down
without hesitation.

My dragons will burn them
to the ground,
my cats will gnaw
on their bones.

And my bats and crows
will always watch over me
and warn me when trespassers
are at my home.

My moat will be manned
by the mightiest dwarfs,
letting no men enter
without the code word.

The women are welcome,
always, for tea,
and also, if needed,
to bury bodies.

I don't ask questions—
it's none of my business—
they would not have struck down
innocent victims.

Oh, designing my castle
with all of its secrets,
where men will be trapped
inside my basement;

it is utter joy, in fact,
there is no excitement that I lack,
my own castle that is packed
with bats and cats and witches' hats.

Scavengers

We hunt them down like scavengers,
we sniff out their toxicity.
It is easy for us to find them, as
they're covered in toxic masculinity.
It is a scent
we will never forget.

We find them lurking in the shadows,
waiting for vulnerable women to walk by.
With their weapons in hand,
they pounce and they strike.
It is a sight
that gives all women fright.

We stake out their hiding places,
those in the light and dark,
as evil has no time stamp
for piercing women's hearts.
It is a wound
we will all know too soon.

The cowards are stalking their prey
unbeknownst that we are now predators,
luring them out from hiding
to send them back to their creator.
It is a mission
that has become our passion.

The only clues we choose to leave
are those that inform other women,
so they may join our pursuit
of making men *our* victims.
It is an undertaking
for which my soul has been aching.

We are the scavengers—the defenders—
of women and girls seeking retribution.
They made us their enemy, and now
it's time for a revolution.
We all win
when we bury evil men.

They may call us their victims,
though we are still standing;
we are now the adversaries
and we are expanding.
As the judge and jury,
we are demanding
a harsher sentence
of the utmost violent.
We are the executioners
remanding them to silence.

I Choose Violence

No more miss nice girl,
I tried that route.
That path is now blocked,
and there's only one way out.

So I sharpen my knives
and slip them into my belt,
no longer concerned for
the wrath they'll be dealt.

I don't have the energy
to impart new teachings;
they didn't do their homework
and I don't give a fuck about their feelings.

I tried kindness.
(I refuse to try weakness.)
I tried to ignore,
but I no longer have patience.

On the path behind me,
I smiled too much—
feigning politeness,
allowing myself to be touched.

And now I slap every hand
and stare daggers with my eyes
anytime a man reaches
and tries to grab as I walk by.

This trail in front of me
is now paved
with thorny branches
and darker days.

Until men learn to leave us alone,
to leave us in peace and silence,
I will carry sharper objects.
I am no longer nice.
I now choose violence.

Queen of (Word) He(ART)s

Oh, the rabbit is late
and I dare not wait,
and so, heads must roll

Men at the gates
spewing their hate
as I quietly sip my tea

My pocket watch ticking
as their screams become deafening
and now I must prepare

The dungeon beneath me
has been feeling quite empty
and begging to be fed

So I gather the trolls
who don't comprehend *no*
and send them to their deaths

For when the rabbit is late
I dare not wait
to be talked off of the ledge…

So, off with their heads!

A Witchy Tea Party

Don't Forget Your Magic

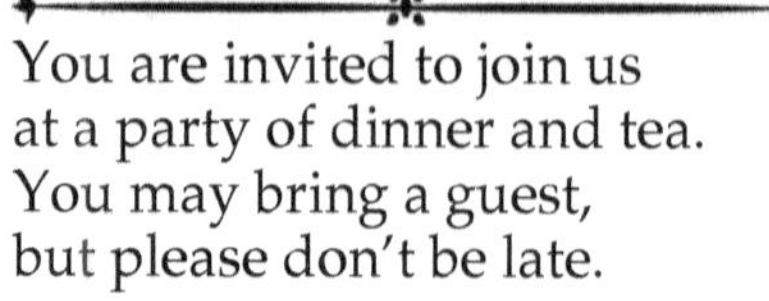

You are invited to join us
at a party of dinner and tea.
You may bring a guest,
but please don't be late.

We must start promptly
before the full moon is high,
so that we may be
in full alignment.

The Mother Universe
will be our guide,
as we enjoy fellowship
through the night.

As we watch
the stars align,
we will have an
experience most divine.

The cauldron has bubbled
for several days,
and it is now time
to take our place

within the trees,
by the graves,
where we honor those
who have left our space.

I hope you can join us
for a party, most epic,
and please do not forget
to bring your magic.

Turning Tables

I'm trying to heal her,
trying to make her proud,
to give her all the reasons
to smile…and to shroud
the let-downs, the disappointments,
the doubt.

She deserves a hero
who believes in her fully.
She deserves a love
that heals her completely.

She deserves the comfort
of a long-lasting hug
full of trust and safety,
reminding her of her worth.

She deserves to hear the words
that stitch up her broken heart,
and to find her solace
in her own written art.

That little girl
I once was,
she deserves to be
fully loved
for who she was then
and who she is now,
and I refuse to let her down.

I had built walls
to protect her in;
though, I realize the damage
that I caused her then.

And so, I have broken
down those walls,
let the light shine in,
as I heed her calls.

She wants to laugh
and play a bit more,
she wants to love
without a worried heart.

And so, I will be her warrior
and her gentle protector,
steering her toward all
life has to offer.

You are My Happiness

You are my favorite
part of each day,
you bring so much joy
to my space.

You are my reason
to wake each morning,
you are my purpose
when skies are grey.

You bring laughter
and ever-lasting comfort,
I would be so lonely
if you never came.

And when I'm hurting
and you curl up on me
you bring solace
I cannot erase.

My adoration for you
cannot be replaced;
I am so thankful
that you stayed.

I hope to reassure you
every single day
that you are cherished
more than I can convey.

I hope you know how
much I love you,
please don't take
my happiness away.

This Little Witch, This Little Cat

This little witch used psychic powers
This little witch used crystals
This little witch brewed potions
This little witch picked herbs

This little witch praised the moon
This little witch praised the sun
This little witch praised the earth
This little witch praised the universe

This little witch used curses
This little witch used spells
This little witch chanted words
to send her enemies to hell

And this little witch
lived to tell their tales.

This little cat had sharp claws
This little cat had cute beans
This little cat had fluffy paws
This little cat had razor sharp teeth

This little cat ran crazy
This little cat preferred to sleep
This little cat was nocturnal
This little cat dreamed sweet

This little cat was curious
This little cat liked to climb
This little cat preferred wet food
This little cat preferred dry

And this little cat
became my whole life.

An Autumn Night

I tap away at the keys—
click, click, click—
and notice the gentle breeze
and the leaves rustling, so thick.
I start to light a fire—
I love the amber glow—
but I'm easily distracted
as I hear tapping on my window.
I peek out to see the raven—
my familiar forevermore—
and the wise old owl perched in the tree,
taking watch over my door.
And then a gentle banging arises
and I open up to find
my black cat arriving
for dinner—just in time.
We unwind together
in front of the fire,
and watch the weaving of webs
by the skilled black spider.
I sip my hot tea
and jot down a love story
to the dark, spooky creatures
and all of their mothers.
As the full moon
reaches full height,
I traipse out to the graveyard
on this dark, cool night;
I whisper my secrets
to all the resting souls,
and lie down on the ground
till sleep takes hold.
As above,
so below,
I'm stuck here in the middle
anchored by a tattered soul.
Though I find peace
amongst the departed—
my soul at ease
where bones are buried.

As I sleep
I dream of a place
where witches dance
in full display;
naught a weary
evil mind in sight,
just joy and laughter
filling up the night.
Where tables are larger
and feasts are shared,
and the best wicked souls
feel love and care.
It is amongst the dead
where I can believe
in a better world
for all beings.
If I shall die here
on this night
in this graveyard
before the light,
may I be swept up
by the moon
inside my dreams—
my own cocoon.
Though if I wake again
on this earth,
may I help other souls
still stuck in this curse.
While winter brings rest,
spring and summer rebirth and growth,
it is the autumn nights
that nourish my soul.

Where the Wild Witches Are

We have different rights
when we cross state lines,
unlike men—
always getting away with shit.

We are *not* free.

But we certainly can be.

In a far away land
away from man,
our sisters gather
and build together.

They plant their herbs,
vegetables, and fruits,
untouched and unbothered
by toxic dudes.

They share their food,
share the labor,
no scores to keep
on who is better.

They help one another through the storms they weather.

No men to help—
nor to hinder;
they dine together
each night for dinner.

And when the moon
is on full display,
they join outside
to dance and play.

They share their stories
of the battles they've faced
and support one another,
for it is not a race.

They bathe in Mother Nature
and enjoy endless peace.
It's a place I truly
yearn to be.

Where witches run wild and free.

We must build more communities
for all the women who
have wilder, untamed hearts
and don't do what they're told to do.

For we will never
ever be free
while men control
our humanity.

If you disobey the laws of man
and refuse to ever bow to them,
may you bring your dark, feral heart
and settle in a place where the wild witches are.

Macabre Souls

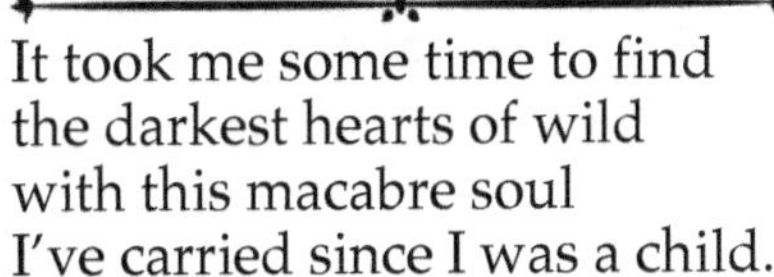

It took me some time to find
the darkest hearts of wild
with this macabre soul
I've carried since I was a child.

I searched far and wide
for the other grim women,
the witchy friends to love me,
knowing my soul was different.

I began to fear
I would never discover
weird companions
like no other.

My journey has been solo
for quite some time,
and all I wanted
was to find

the women that society
claims are most dreadful,
the macabre souls, unearthly,
appalling, and clever.

And as I found
my own true self,
I came upon the creatures
who know me best.

Whispers from the Universe

The messages are delivered
to us by the wind,
from the stars in the sky,
from our long-ago kin.

Their energy in the air
all around us,
their souls surrounding
as they guide us.

We are often
far too loud
to hear their words,
drowning out the sound

in which they speak
from afar,
trying so desperately
to reach our hearts.

We go about our
earthly lives,
as if no longer connected
to those who died.

But our soul companions
are far wiser than we,
returned to the stars
as we continue on hopelessly.

I want so badly
to reconnect,
to hear their guidance,
to feel them next

to me as I
march on
through this life
where I don't belong.

This stop for me is only temporary
and I hope to be returned
to the stars
within their arms
when my time here is done.

Protect Her Heart

We are not damsels
who need to be saved.
We have rescued ourselves
from men for centuries.

We seek out partners
humble and true
who can keep us steady
when we are unsure.

We will not be locked
inside of their cage
waiting for them to swoop in
and lie to our face.

We seek true warriors
who honor the women
who never cower
who never give in.

A loyal partner
to have our backs,
not an alpha male
controlling the pack.

We don't seek *nice* guys—
their *nice* has limits;
we seek eternal kindness
toward all women and children.

Not a man to protect us
when he's had a good day,
then turns on a dime
when he is enraged.

We will not settle
for weak coward leaders.
We pave our own path, and that
is where they shall meet us.

I'm not burning the haystack
to find a needle
hiding within
a bundle of men,
a bundle of evil.

If they want to protect us,
they must know what
they're protecting us from.
Men—like them—hiding
in plain sight
amongst the herd.

We don't trust them
because they all look the same.
Though, they are outnumbered
and they are to blame.

I don't want your *nice*,
I demand you fight
against the toxicity
claiming our lives.

No, love is not a fairytale,
and it's certainly not a game.
I will walk the solo path until
one protects my heart,
protects my name.

Dreamy Ever After

I opened a book and fell right in.
Now I may never get out again.

I'm skipping and hopping
through the trees,
down a wicked path
that leads
to a little danger,
to a big adventure,
never knowing which way
I'll take to get there.

I stare up at mountains
that appear too high,
and then I step forward
and I climb
until I reach the very top,
and just like that…
I jump!

Into the icy cold water below,
submerged so deep,
chilled to my bones,
until I surface yet again,
climb on out
only to begin
to take off on a new trek—
no idea where I'm going yet.

I could climb a tree
and sit with the birds,
listen to them sing
as I learn the words,
or climb inside the
sleeping bears' den
to snuggle up close
and hibernate with them.

And when I awake
from my winter slumber,
I can join the dwarfs
in the forest for supper,
where we enjoy
our chats and laughs
and share stories
of our past.

And as I fall asleep
underneath the moon,
I never have to worry
if I am safe from harm,
because in my storybook
dreamland,
women are always safe
from men.

Maybe that is where
my soul will go
when I am ready
to leave my earthly home—
trapped forever deep inside
a fairytale story
where I feel most alive.

Persephone's Underground Wonderland

Persephone lay down
with a book by the tree,
rested her head
on the trunk with ease.
The story she was reading
told of women in power—
a fictional tale, they say—
the men in their towers.

As she slipped into
her own dreamland,
Persephone met
a brave woman
who invited her
to join her cause—
to tear apart evil
with their own claws.

Persephone noticed
just then and there
daggers extending
straight from her hands.
After the shock,
she smiled a big grin,
for she now had the tools
to root out all the sin.

The women set off
down their own rabbit hole
to mutilate the evil men who said
we must do as we're told.
These women follow
no laws of man;
they rip out their throats
with their bare hands.

Oh, it may sound disturbing—
and definitely gory—
but evil men do not win
in Persephone's story.

She becomes the ruler
of the underground,
ending men's lives
without a sound.

She may even sometimes sic
her own underground hounds
with all of their heads and teeth
onto the men's towns.
Though she also loves
to do her own bidding,
crafting their names
into poisonous venom,
so that they may never
be spoken of again,
as there is no space here
for evil to win.

Persephone found
her own place on her throne,
in her underground wonderland
amongst the bones.
And while she dreams wickedly
book in lap, beneath the tree,
she crafts her own adventure,
she finds her own peace.

A Witch's Winter Night

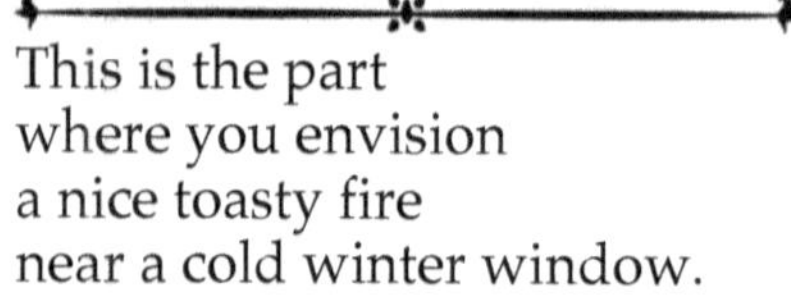

This is the part
where you envision
a nice toasty fire
near a cold winter window.

A steaming cup
of hot cocoa or tea
warming your hands
as you look out on the street.

The night is still
and silent,
with the exception of
the ravens

as they mew
through the night,
a sound that gives you
comfort and delight.

As the fire is
winding down,
you pull on your
cozy night gown

and tuck yourself—
and your cats—
into bed for witchy
dreams goodnight.

Little Old Witch Who Lived in a Shoe

I'd rather be
the little old lady
house full of cats—
them thinking I'm lonely—
than to be
broken into pieces
that fit into their society.

I'll build the shelves
to hold all my books,
and all the cat towers
where the felines can rest.
I will put on a pot of tea,
and invite my friends
to dine with me.

And we will enjoy
so many laughs,
and secrets,
and stories,
and lift each other up.

Oh my, this is sounding
really quite nice—
it sounds like a dream—
a quiet peaceful life.

If it means peace
to die alone in my home
with all of my cats
and a house full of love,
I can think of far,
far worse ways
to live my life;
so, give me alone any day.

A Dreamy Ride

Come along for this
dreamy ride;
I'll paint you a story
of a blissful life.

Carriages that never
turn back into pumpkins,
shoes that never slip off
as you are running.

Your prince will never
not recognize you—
no need to make you
try on a lost shoe.

The tea parties never
have to end
when you are enjoying
your time with friends.

Your animal companions
protect you in the forest,
and trolls never charge you
to cross the bridges.

Peace is in abundance
and evil cannot reign,
because all of the people
refuse to bow to them.

Happiness is not driven
by how much one owns,
it is always felt
within our very bones.

And oh, this ride
has no stops;
though it rises,
it never drops.

It is a blissful
teacup ride,
spinning up
a beautiful life.

An Untea Party

My tears are for the women
who just wanted to be believed,
who faced unfathomable violence,
and watched their predator go free.

No one listened as they screamed,
and no one helped them as they bled.
Jail time would just ruin the men's lives—
justice never granted to the innocent.

So, if they will not listen
and protect all women,
we will no longer plead.

Instead, we shall invite them over for tea.

An untea party is just
what we need
to lure them in
and watch them scream.

If they want to
hunt women down,
we will wait for them
as we sit around

the table that is set
with little surprises
for all the men.

Take a bite of biscuit,
wash it down with tea.
As their vision goes blurry,
we'll be the last thing they see.

We no longer wait for justice.
We no longer beg for peace.
We will set the table
and let them sip our tea.

I Choose Me

Since I was a child,
I knew I was different.
I always had this *thing*…
I could feel it.
My love for animals,
my unwavering empathy;
I felt far too deeply
for someone who hadn't hit puberty.

Children and animals
have always been drawn to me.
Though it was a feeling of pride,
it also felt heavy—
a purpose to protect,
a lifelong burden.

I tried to do it all—
save the children,
rescue the animals.
I tried to be the person
who gave and gave
endlessly.

And still, I feel
it was never enough.
There is always someone
out there who will judge—
someone who will say
I didn't do enough.

I carried the expectations
of others for far too long,
believing I needed their approval
to be seen as "good".
Though all of the good
is automatically cancelled
as soon as I slip up
and forget to be perfect.

And it took me some time
to realize
that
is simply not worth it.

I now surround myself
with others who
do not keep tally
or accuse,
friends who remind me
that I am loved
even on the days
I can't offer much.

I no longer have to
jump through hoops
or bleed myself dry
and keep being used
by people who claim
they love me as-is,
and then get mad
when I don't fit
into the box they made for me.
No, I will never be who they want me to be.

That little girl who did
everything right,
no longer exists
and now she fights
back against
the expectations,
the societal norms;
she does not care about
the opinions that are formed.

There is more solace
and comfort in
becoming who I want
no matter what.
So, if I must lose
people who
do not like
who I'm turning into,
I will bask in my peace
knowing I love who I choose to be.

A Kind Witch

I am a kind witch.

I am not a nice witch.

Do not mistake

my kindness for weakness.

Cross the witch,

cross the boundaries,

find yourself

fucking drowning.

I am kind to those in need,

not lonely men out on the street.

Do not fucking cross me.

And now that that's out of the way,

have yourself a lovely day.

My kindness is reserved for those

who leave women the fuck alone.

Spread the Love

One person's sadness
does not need to be
greater than yours
to be believed.

We are all carrying
ghosts no one sees.
So, just be kind;
things are extra heavy.

We need to throw
a little more
magic around
to help the poor.

We need to lift
more women up
and not let men
drain our cups.

We need to teach the children
to believe
that happiness is never
out of reach.

We need more kindness
sprinkled around,
easing the heavy burdens
we're all carrying around.

We need more witches
chanting spells
of hope and love—
magic lingering in our cells.

And may we see more
evil men fall
from their thrones
where they try to rule all.

May the stories we tell,
and those we read,
make us all
believe

that evil and hate
and greed
never, ever
fully succeed,

because love
always wins.
So, spread a little more
into this world we're in.

And in the end,
may we all gather
together within our own
happily ever after.

The Witch's Cottage

I crave a space
where I can be
free to dream
free to breathe;
a place somewhere
within the trees
a little garden
a peaceful stream.

A spot tucked away
from the hate and crime.
That is what
I want to find.
A place dreamed up
inside my mind.
A cottage of hope
that is truly mine.

A hidden room
behind my shelves
where I can craft
and I can spell;
plenty of room
for plenty of animals
where love abounds
and comfort dwells.

A safe place for
my friends to rest
and enjoy the things
we love best;
crafting, chatting,
making a mess
and laughing loudly
with aching chests.

A little plot where
we all gather
where love and friendship
is all that matters;
where food is abundant
and we dine together
where we share stories
that make the world better.

Believe in Magic

If you can dream it,
then you can believe it.
If you can believe it,
then you can achieve it.

There is no limit
to what you can do.
Never, ever stop
speaking your truth.

Do as you please,
as long as you don't harm others,
unless you are fighting back
against the monsters.

Seek out your own path,
no need to follow the crowd.
Do not hide who you are;
always love loud.

Some mountains may seem
a bit too high,
but you were made from the stars,
and so you come from the sky.

No river is too deep
for you to swim.
Do not let the fear
of danger win.

Often times, we discover
who we truly are
when we battle the villains
and walk through the fire.

Always keep your
head held high.
The patriarchy will not
win this fight.

Stand up,
stand proud,
stand tall,
speak loud.

When you believe it,
wishes come true.
Shooting stars
or candles will do.

So, make your wish
and let it fly.
The magic within you
will never die.

Jane and Jill

Jane and Jill
went up the hill
leaving Jack behind.

Jack found out,
went to hunt them down,
not knowing what he'd find.

The trail they left
was made of blood,
not breadcrumbs like
Hansel and Gretel.

He moved forward
cautiously
to prove he had
enough mettle.

He found them there
in the forest
surrounding the cauldron
and fire,

dancing, chanting,
laughing,
as their spells would
soon be transpired.

As Jack neared closer
a small branch snapped
as he crept in to see.

Jane and Jill smirked,
but did not turn,
for then Jack might flee.

They knew their plan
had worked quite well,
the sacrifice now arrived.

It was time to throw
the final ingredient in…
burning Jack alive.

Soul Food

I carry around the soul
of a witch who has lived many lives,
died many deaths,
and still, somehow, survived.
The soul of a woman
who has more battles to fight,
more innocent to protect,
more lessons to find.
This soul must be in search of
something far greater
than this evil, cruel world—
maybe *she* is the savior.
Jesus, the man, was crucified, too,
simply for loving his neighbors—
for being *too* good.
While I do carry
kindness in my soul,
I also carry vengeance
that will soon unfold.
I do not claim myself a saint,
or a goddess worthy of anyone
groveling at my feet.
I do not seek recognition
for my heroic deeds;
I only want to serve the rich
so that we may all have
a plentiful feast.
So, gather 'round, friends,
let's make a toast
so that we may nourish
our weak, withered bones.
I do not fear the consequences,
for my soul will never rest;
until the evil is consumed,
the rich we will ingest.

Stay Feral

When they tell you to smile
show them your teeth
grit them together
and fucking scream.

As soon as they touch you
bark like a dog
don't forget to growl and snarl
until you've run them off.

When they get super angry
respond with "Oh, buddy, big feelings"
remind them to seek therapy for daddy
issues with which they're dealing.

When they're following
too close behind
stop dead in your tracks
and stare them down wide-eyed.

Oh, and remind them that you fucking bite.

Kindness will no longer do
we tried that long enough.
We are now choosing violence
when they touch us.

Pull out your stun gun
and your self-defense ring.
Always keep a knife handy;
it's fun to watch them bleed.

I get that "no" may be
too large a word for them to grasp
so I suggest they study up
because their lesson is coming fast.

Safety first, don't forget
to wear gloves for your hands
to protect your knuckles
as you beat the shit out of him.

This is what we must do now
to keep ourselves alive;
staying wild and feral
is how we will survive.

Oh, and be sure to show them how a woman really fights.

Wayward

I seek out the weirdos,
the outcasts, the witches;
I seek out the
wayward women.
The ones who cannot
be governed or predicted,
those a bit wanton
with depraved inclinations.

We shall continue to be
difficult to control,
or rather,
impossible, really.

Unpredictable.
Perverse.
Capricious.

These are the women I choose as sisters.

Feral.
Wild.
Untamed.

That is how you inherit the Wayward name.

We shall forever do it our own way.

Made. Of. Magic.

Hey mama, I know
you need to escape for a bit;
the kids finally in bed
and you now get to sit

Put up your feet
(and forget the dishes)
take a bath, if you can
(really, forget the dishes)

The kids are breathing
and soundly sleeping,
it's okay to give yourself
some healing

May you always be
reminded
that your role matters;
we need more like you
to raise the littles
in hopes one day
the world will be better

Turn off the news,
it's meant to confuse,
to make you panic,
to frighten you

Do not let that
get the better of you

You've got the most
important job to do

Tuck them in
while they still let you,
read them a story…
or maybe two

And when it's
your time to rest,
please, just leave
the fucking dishes

And never forget
you were Made Of Magic

A Poetic Death

A sword to the heart
to save your true love.
Poisonous concoctions
so you both leave this earth.
Leaping right
in front of a bus
to push another
to safety first.

A hand slipping away
as you fall off the edge.
The last final "I love you"
with your dying breath.
All of the joys in life
flashing through your head
as you finally meet
your final rest.

I've died a million ways
inside my head.
Though when reality
finally sets in,
I am certain I will die
alone with my cats,
and there may not be
much of me left
once they find my body
after my poetic death.

The Woods are for Women

Since they are no longer good
for building us cabins in the woods,
and the only time they spend out there
is hunting creatures without a care,
and women are still choosing the bear,
we shall reclaim our sacred space—
the forest, the animals, and the trees;
that is *our* peace.

So men, leave it be.

The woods are no longer meant for you,
they're for the women hunting you.
We now grow claws and vampire teeth
to capture you for our wicked tea party.
Such a delight to dine under the moon
after sacrificing men in *our* woods.

Paintbrush Writer

I'm painting a picture inside my mind,
within my brain canvas,
since I cannot draw in real-life.

Sometimes I see the artwork
laid out right inside my eyes
before the words are formed.

And other times, the words
find me first,
and then the visual is born.

The words are my paintbrush
constructing a vision,
building the pieces,
projecting an image.

And then I take those
pretty—and wicked—scenes
and turn them into
poetry.

I see a table
set for tea
and witchy women
surrounding me.

And then I see
the rabbit run by,
and I am led away
by surprise,
as the mad cat
calls to me
from his perch
within his tree;
though, I am too busy
to ask what he needs.

The pictures play out
like a movie
within my temple—
fast and slowly.

Sometimes the projector
is flickering,
making it difficult for me
to write anything.

Like a pinball machine,
my thoughts are the ball
bouncing around
hitting the walls.

And I try my best
to wrangle them in,
to write the words
as fast as I can
to tell the stories
stuffed within my head—
a never-ending task
with no rest.

So, if my thoughts and words
reach your hands, your eyes, your ears,
do know that they were brewed
from the many images that appeared
inside my mind as I watched—
sometimes getting utterly lost.

Somehow those stories
reached the page,
spilled from the ink
as I raced
to get them down
before they were lost;
as writers know,
we are only the paintbrush.

Macabre Wonderland

I am not falling down the rabbit hole,
I am happily climbing right in;
for there is art inside the dark,
and a new adventure is set to begin!

There is the blackest Cheshire cat
waiting for me in the tree—
grinning quite evilly—
and a cauldron brewing tea.

I am draped beneath my silk robe,
waiting for their arrival;
I fear that they will hesitate,
and the Mad Hatter hates it
when we are late.

The potion bottles all around,
spell books covering the table;
I want to take a quick peek,
but the mad cat is watching—
and talking—distracting me.

Now that we have all gathered here
at this midnight hour,
we can begin the ritual
for holding all the power.

Though outsiders will tell a fib,
claiming we are evil;
they do not understand
what they do not know,
they do not comprehend
that we mean no harm.

The power we want…
is from the stars,
not from money, or hatred,
or greed—
but power to help those in need.

And if we must eat the rich
to drown out all of their lies,
well, that is what we shall do,

hiding out of sight
in this macabre wonderland
on this wicked night.

A Toast

A toast to the monsters
who did not succeed
in controlling me
and watching me bleed

A toast to their failures
as they go to sleep each night,
may their own demons
eat them alive

A toast to their cruelty,
may it swallow them whole,
leaving them with nothing—
not even their soul

May each transgression
they ever fulfilled
be the very reason
that gets them killed

And a toast to Karma,
our very best friend,
helping us to take down
all of the evil men

Wicked Mad Tea Party

A sip for you,
a sip for me,
it is so nice
to meet for tea.

Tell me your stories
of how you went mad,
and I'll share all the
wicked dreams I've had.

The world is too weak
for our power,
as we share our schemes
and we empower

all of the little girls
in our stories;
and we strip them of
their fears and worries

of evil men
hunting them down,
for we will teach them
how to stand their ground.

We'll invite them for tea
and teach them the spells
that will send their enemies
straight to hell.

We will also tell
tales of whimsy—
not *always* gory,
not always cringey.

Oh, my dear friend,
it is so nice to catch up;
would you like some sugar
inside your cup?

One lump
or two?

What's bothering
you?

You seem quite distracted.

I know it's not
a full moon tonight,
but you do not need to hide
your wicked light.

Please, do share
your madness with me;
that is exactly why
we meet for tea.

The bats are flying
from their caves,
the skeletons are rising
from their graves
and the cats are creeping
through the night,
as the owls guard over us
from the trees up high.

We are quite
protected here
in the woods,
so have no fear.

What is it you are holding back?

Is it some purpose that you lack?

Do not you worry,
I will protect your secrets,
help you bury the bodies—
I'm sure they deserved it.

And I know just the place!

Let us go and dig the graves.

Do not fret, dear friend.
Evil men deserve this end.

And when we're done,
we'll meet again,
under the weeping willow,
we will dine as friends
and enjoy another
pot of tea.

I simply love a wicked mad tea party!

Can't Go Back to Yesterday

A Different Person Then

The day you died
is when life felt real.
No more protector,
no more daddy's little girl.

She vanished as quickly as you did.

I didn't know the words to say
as I stood there staring at your pale face
inside that casket they lay you in,
never to hug your neck again.

A loss like that feels tremendous
when you're just a child.
And the questions unanswered
drove my mind quite wild.

It all filled up inside my head,
the whys and what-ifs...
the "what did I do
to deserve this?"

When everyone is grieving,
where does one turn
to seek the comfort,
to heal the hurt?

Instead you box it all up,
tucked inside
a tiny mind,
a girl unsure
how to navigate this world.

And as the sadness
fills up within
the tiny body
I am trapped in,
it flows over,
turning into anger—
and I'm called a bitch,
and I can't take this,
all I did wrong
was lose my father!

No one to help me navigate this.

And so I ran far away
from the little girl I was that day
that my father left this place…

I can't go back to yesterday.

When you lose your protector,
you lose your safety,
and people now think
they can berate you,
simply because they don't think
you'll stand up for yourself—
they think you're weak.

And you go through the motions,
try to follow the rules,
even though you're broken
and everything hurts.
This is just too much
for a sad, lost little girl.

Sculpted into a warrior
to protect myself,
no longer hiding
or scared of death,
running toward danger,
thinking I'll find all the answers.

I lost myself on that day,
when I stared into your face
no longer here, just a body
lying there, nothing inside it.

It took a while,
but now I see,
I carried you with me
on that day.

I believe I'm alive
because of your protection—
not necessarily the ending
that I wanted or dreamed of,
but I am Me because of your love.

And Daddy, I am finding her again,
your little bag lady,
I'm finding her grin.

I've done it all—hit every goal
I set for myself to fill up the holes
that were left behind
on the day my innocence died.

I am not quite where
I'm going yet,
but I found my own way
and took my own path.

I do believe I would be
somewhere—someone—
else entirely
if you were still here today.

I still miss you, though I do think
I've become who I am
because you left that day—
giving me a fighting chance
to live my life fully,
not needing a man.

And so, I thank you for that.

And I hope you can peacefully rest,
let go of the anger that always held you back.
You also did not deserve the start you had.
Though you weren't perfect, I still love you, Dad.

Thank you for being my biggest fan
when I was just a little kid.

Your life cut short just past forty,
and I am now older than you were.
I was lost for quite some time,
but I never lost sight of her—

that little girl you found so smart,
the one you held so dear;
I am her protector now.
I can take it from here.

Changing Mirrors

I stare into the mirror
at a different version of myself—
more lines grace my face
like poetry,
more color than a rainbow.

Am I who I want to be?
Or am I hiding in this skin
which I have adorned
with jewels and words
and artwork?

Am I becoming who
I'm supposed to be…
or someone I never believed
I deserved to be?

The mirror doesn't hide
the scars, the tears,
the loss, the fear.
It highlights it all
like a map of my existence.

The mirror does not lie,
though it reflects a new story
each time I take a peek.

Sometimes I pause for a moment
to read it all.
And sometimes I look away
as quickly as I can.

The mirror is neither
friend nor foe,
but a looking glass
of past, present,
and an uneasy future.

What obstacles of broken glass
await me?

What treasures am I bound
to find…
and miss?

My mirror does not tell me stories
of the fairest of them all.
It places pain on full display
and reminds me that life
is fleeting.

This very image of me—
as I am now—
is only for an instant.
Once I look away,
I will change.
When I return,
I won't be the same.

Mirror, mirror on the wall,
protect me from society's call
to become someone for which
they approve;
please do not let me lose
sight of who I have always been.

Please, show me the joy
I had as a kid…
before the world changed me.

Transformation

I feel it.
Deep inside my bones.
Piercing through my soul.

My eyes are wide open.
My mind a medley of possibility.
Endless possibilities.

Just as the caterpillar turns into a moth
(or a butterfly if your soul is light;
my soul is a bit darker),

I see the pieces of Her behind me.
The girl I started as,
the woman I was before,
the woman I'm leaving behind
like a shell,
and becoming the woman who dares to
be that little girl again.

With peace in my heart.
With knowledge in my bones.
With wisdom in my soul.
With eyes for all that was taken when she
was no longer innocent.

I see her again.
She's always been there,
tucked away,
boxed in,
reigned in,
hidden.
Hidden but watching—
don't speak unless spoken to.

But she is here.
Her voice.
Her power.
Her wide-eyed wonder for all of the
beauty she once saw in the world.

She recognizes the dark in the world.
She remains committed to helping those
in need.
And she chooses her own peace above
all else.

She says goodbye to the woman in the
mirror behind her—
the woman who did not see purpose in a
simple breath—
and turns toward the mirror in front,
shining with a radiance of which only that
once little girl could give off.

I see her.
She sees me.
We move forward together,
with wonder and curiosity.

She no longer cares if her light is blinding.

She is here.
Transformed.

Elevation

I did the work.
I climbed the mountain.
I sweat, and cried, and bled.

Not a man alive
who can get me
off
this pedestal.

I believed in myself,
cheered myself on,
picked myself back up
each time I would fall.

No one there to save me
when I needed loving arms.
So, I trained myself
to weather the storms.

I fought the battles on my own,
bought myself my own home,
cared for the helpless in their time of need,
and kept myself safe from hate and greed.

Each time I falter,
I always rise,
and I will keep standing
until I die.

This level I have put myself on—
above the clouds in my tower—
is elevated well beyond
where anyone can take my power.

A New Future

I am swimming in thoughts
and words,
in dreams
and plans
and aspirations…
just on the other end
of the horizon.

The light at the end
of the tunnel
is blinding;
I just want to stay
in my dark cave
hiding.

Though I know
I won't
make it out
alive,
I may as well
enjoy the ride.

So, I suppose,
I should hit
a few more
goals;
write more words,
release more books,
more stories
I wished to read
as a girl.

I may be banned
by toxic men,
but I will lead
the women's
resistance—
always
reminding them,
we *can* win it.
We open our
own jars,
hang up our
own shelves,
pay our
own bills;
we don't need
their help.

So, if they
are so lonely—
an epidemic,
I'm told—
maybe they
should try
smiling
a bit more.

There is no
need to dwell
on the past—
an eternal hell
for women
controlled
by violent
men.

We aren't doing
that shit again.

And so, we must
all move
forward
toward
a future where
we coexist.

And if men
don't like it,
well,
that's tough shit.

Lyrical Lullabies

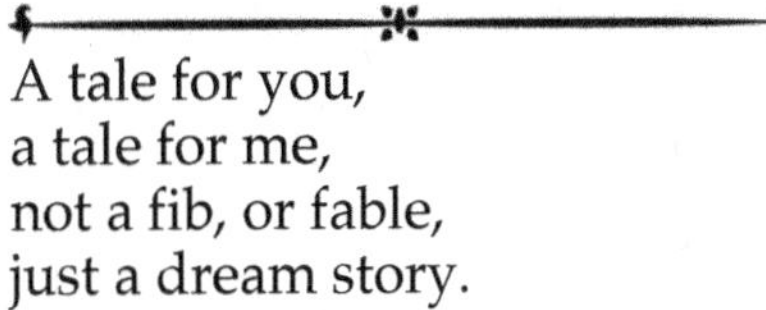

A tale for you,
a tale for me,
not a fib, or fable,
just a dream story.

A lullaby I'd like to weave.

A little girl dances
beneath the moon,
no fear of boys
being cruel to her.

A great big sky
full of stars,
as she wishes
on every one.

And every birthday candle
that she blows out
delivers her desires
to the clouds.

And she is always safe
inside her bed,
inside her home,
and inside her own head.

The monsters will never
break down her door,
but she will take them food
when they're hungry and poor.

Her smile lights up
the great, big sky,
and she always dreams
sweetly every night.

There are no bedbugs
in her bed,
and she is always
surrounded by friends.

Where wild things are,
and goodnight moon,
and three little bears
tuck Goldilocks in, too.

The hungry caterpillar
never steals
from the poor and helpless
just to get his fill.

Where Charlotte's web
is always spun
inside the corner
watching over her.

Where Charlie's chocolate
is always shared
and the secret garden
is never bare.

Where Wendy
chooses to
never, ever
grow up too soon.

And Peter, the rabbit,
is always waiting
to meet Alice in her
wonderland setting.

These lyrical lullabies
are for that same little girl
that you tucked away,
so, look inward, girl.

I Must Believe

I believe in the clouds
I believe in the sky
I believe in the beauty
I see through my eyes
I believe in the stars
I believe in the moon
I believe that we are always
gone too soon
I believe in the sun
I believe in the trees
I believe we, as humans
are inferior to bees
I believe in rainbows
I believe in love
and I believe we can all
rise above
the cruelties we're facing
all over our planet—
innocent creatures suffering
so the rich can own it
I believe humanity
is far better than we see
within the news we watch
within the comments we read
I believe that if we all gather
and rise up against
those in power
we will be victorious
and we can live a life
more glorious
than the one capitalism built
I *must* believe—we all have to
before humanity dies
and our planet wilts

Little Monsters

The little monsters are at it again—
it could be cats or dogs or kids—
but we are all mothers
to the innocent.

Let them get their zoomies on,
playing and jumping and having fun;
for far too soon they will grow old
and we will miss the chaotic home.

Slipping and sliding, learning their world,
discovering wonders they can unfurl,
never knowing when they'll stop—
exhausted from all of the lessons taught.

As they tire and climb in our laps,
we are so very thankful for their naps,
for soon they will begin again…
and maybe next time we'll join in.

There is no feeling more special
than being a safe space for their tussles,
so that they may always know
how to stand up and defend their own.

And when they snuggle up together,
our hearts, they melt, for it is far better
when their love is shared with others;
that is the gift we give as mothers.

Mothers

They say I am not a mother
because I don't have my own children,
but they don't say the same
to women who adopt the orphans.

Just because my kids have paws
and tiny, little dagger claws,
I still know each one by their own sound,
a mother's instinct tightly bound

within my soul;
all women know
that fierce protector
that lives in our bones.

I take care of them
all night and day,
watching them sleep,
watching them play.

I worry when
they don't feel well,
and feel so guilty
when I choose to yell.

They seek me out
when they are scared.
I provide comfort
full of care.

I teach them things
they need to learn,
even if they rarely listen—
cats are so stubborn.

I will protect them
with my life.
My heart will *never* recover
when they're no longer alive.

I provide them food
so they grow big and strong.
So, yes, I really am
their mom.

Imprint

I didn't know how much I needed you
until you finally arrived,
like a long-lost companion
I forgot about for a while.

You pounced right in
and shook things up
within my life,
within my home.

You nestled to sleep
within my arms,
a sound slumber knowing
you were safe from harm.

You showed me love.
You showed me trust.
As your personality shined,
you showed me how much fun

it can be to have
kittens around.
And I couldn't just stop
at only one.

I was a dog mom
before you appeared;
though, I quickly remembered
how I always held cats so dear.

I felt it the moment
you imprinted on me.
And I knew instantly,
you were always meant for me.

Change of Plans

We make the plans
and go about our day,
checking off tasks and rerouting
when things get in our way.

We attempt to foresee
all the obstacles ahead
and try to prepare for
the countless moments of dread.

We think we have time
to figure it out,
to make the right moves,
to remove the doubt.

All the people outside
send judgements and opinions
that we never asked for,
as if our choices are their business.

We try to do the right thing
no matter the outcome
and limit our own happiness
just to feel a little loved.

And the people watching
do nothing but judge.

And so, I no longer care
what anyone thinks
about the life I have chosen
or the decisions I make

about my own life
and how I will live it—
alone with five cats
and saving the innocent.

The Universe steers me
in the direction I'm headed;
not all goes to plan
and I'm okay with it.

The Universe has
plans of Her own.
I'm just Her vessel
until She calls me home.

Banned

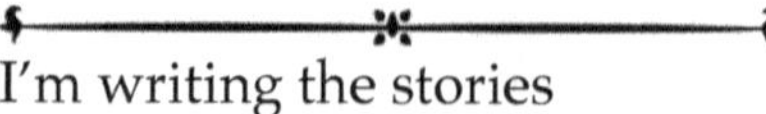

I'm writing the stories
they don't want me to tell

I'm turning my rage
into art

Painting a picture
they want to ban

so terrified that
I will impart

my knowledge of man
into little girls' minds

the evil they spew
exposing their lies

But Lilith didn't kneel
and neither will I

It is far past time
they pay for their crimes

So, I'm writing the stories
they want to keep hidden

of the witchy women
defeating evil villains

and the witches always win…

So, be sure to pick up
a few library books
that they have tried to ban.

Everyday Superwoman

If you've ever cried yourself to sleep,
waking to face another day
in which you must keep
all of your ducks in a row,
then you must know
inside each of us
is a superhero.

Our magic is our strength,
our power is our resolve
to always make ends meet
even if we must do it alone.

The world has tried
to knock us down,
and we keep rising
from the ground
to do it all again,
wondering if we
will ever win.

But please, remember,
it is not a game
that we win or lose,
and it's not a race.

We do not have to compete
with anyone else,
as so many of us are struggling.

After your long, weary day
is done,
and you finally get to rest
your bones,
tuck yourself in
at night,
and remind yourself
why you fight.

We all have a cause,
we all have a reason.
Women were made to
be superheroes,
that is why we
are all breathing.

Poet and I Know It

Don't mind me
if I randomly speak
in poet

It is a language
many have heard
but don't know it

Where words connect
and feel like home
as they slip off of my tongue

A lyrical stream
of steady rhythm
enveloping me

A safe space to land
within my own head
when emotions are never-ending

A rhyme for a friend
to remind her again
that she holds her own power

there in her hands
and within her soul,
where her magic is devoured

It is far easier for me
to believe
my own words when they flow

So, don't mind me
if I randomly speak
in poet, as I do know

that I was simply made
for this,
words rhyming
as they slip

onto the pages before me
as I craft my own
fairytale stories

Free at Last

I'm honestly ready to go
at any time;
not meant to be sad,
for I've had a full life.
I accomplished goals
I never expected;
I set out on adventures
that should have been scary.
I've faced down evil
and said countless
goodbyes;
I feel like I have lived
numerous lives—
full of hardship
and too much strife.
I have battled
through the storms,
paved my own way,
made my own rules.
I have tripped
and I have fallen;
my body has adorned
so many bruises.
Wounds have stitched
inside my soul,
and I have known
friendship
that has made me feel
whole.
I have held a hand
as it left this earth;
I have watched a mother
as she gave birth.

I have rescued animals
who had lost all hope—
and children, too,
who weren't safe at home.
I have helped many
in more need than I;
I have filled
up my life.

And so, I am not afraid
to say goodbye.
I am craving the rest
I have been denied;
my bones are weary,
as is my mind.
No, death is nothing
for me to fear,
for I have consumed
so much
in forty years.

My heart wasn't meant
for such a cruel world
that has taken more from
me
than I can afford.
If my time to go
is somewhere near,
my heart and mind
will finally be free from
here.

Somewhere Over the Castle

Somewhere
over the castle
where fields are green,
there is beauty
as far as the eye
can see.

Instead of
running
through the meadows,
we are stuck in a 9-5.
And it often
feels like
we won't get out
alive.

Out in the
pasture,
the animals
roam free,
though they are
also affected
by our
human greed.

Somewhere
over the riches
flowers bloom,
they are our
reminder
we must grow
up too soon.

And when we
get stuck
in the hustle,
and buried
in bills to pay,
we often forget
we were not
meant
to live
this way.

And so,
I wish
upon the stars,
to wake up
where the greed
is far
behind
me.

And traipse again
within the grass,
where dandelion
wishes
always last,

and night
is safe
from evil
men
and the
patriarchy
never wins…

That's where
you'll find
me.

As I lay
myself to rest,
I wish for more
and for the best
for all the people
behind
me.

They deserve
far better
than this,
though greed
is the wish
on human lips.
I'm not certain
I was born
for this.

It is too
dark here
for me.

But somewhere
over the castle,
freedom lies.
Peace and love
in abundance,
no more hate
and crime.

And if I must
awake each day
in this awful
light,
I will wish
upon the moon
as I chase
my dreams
each night.

Out the Other Side

Dodging traumas and
obstacles we face
as we go through
this race
we call life

Filled with pain,
and madness,
and strife

And eventually we
must realize
you cannot escape your past

You must go through it
if you are to last

No, in this wonderland,
you cannot go back

Press through the darkness,
as your lanterns flicker

Watch your step,
as snakes do slither

everywhere we walk
and tread

never knowing which
are poisonous

Keep your wits about you
and keep moving ahead

There is only forward;
behind you is dead

And one day, the light
will poke through

from the other side
where you're heading to

We all have different
trails to take

to reach the side
where hope awaits

So, do not give in,
though you should take breaks

And I promise you,
we will celebrate

once we all reach the beauty
on the other side

We *will* make it,
dead or alive

SIN(cerely)

It was a knock,
I know that it was;
but nothing was there
when I went to look.

There are creatures outside
I want to let in,
even though I've been warned
it would be a sin.

I am quite tempted
to open the window
just a crack
for just a minute.

After all,
I'd love to feel
the autumn breeze
give my arms a chill.

But the kingdom
cautioned us so well,
conditioned to be lulled
into their spell.

They have me scared
to be sent to hell
if I open my eyes
and see the world.

Though, I heard a knock,
I swear I did;
it would be quite silly
not to open it.

After all,
the moon is there
watching over me,
so if I dare

take a quick
small peek,
to see what's outside
waiting for me.

It could be danger,
it could be pain,
or it could be freedom
to live in sin's name.

I pack a basket,
pull my cloak from the hook,
jot down a quick letter
and grab a book.

"Goodbye."
It read.

Just that one word.

Except for the signature
which read,

SIN(cerely),
Not Yours

The Kindest Prince

Kiss the frog,
find the prince.
Here we go
with this shit again.

Frogs can be friends;
men can't do that shit.

They don't event understand "No"
is a full sentence.

Judged for our lips,
our hair, and our skin,
though they lose their shit
when we share stories of men

who have proved to us
time and again
they cannot be trusted,
and we cannot win.

I hope one day to tell a new tale
of a man who sought therapy
and healed himself.

He will not pull up
on a pure white steed;
he will be giving back
to the innocent in need.

He will rule himself
in a gentle way;
he will share his story
as we grow each day.

He will not rescue me,
nor will I him;
we will protect one another—
perhaps, become best friends.

Though I know they are out there,
I'm not hunting them down,
as I've found my own peace
inside my own house.

But if my happily ever after
shall include a man,
may he be the kindest person
in all of the land.

Broken Looking Glass

I gazed into the looking glass
hoping to see something other
than a broken past—
perhaps a dream
that could still come true;
but the only thing looking back
was the empty darkness
of loss and uncertainness,
and I'm just stuck here
with hopelessness.

A shattered mirror
brings bad luck,
and here I am
completely stuck
peering into the shards,
wondering how many
times my poor heart
can be broken
and utterly bruised—
full of scars,
full of wounds.

I must protect it,
wrap it up tight
inside a bandage
away from the light,
bound up soundly
deep inside,
covered up,
safe from lies.

Too much treachery
crossed its path—
a road less taken,
filled with wrath,
and I don't even
know the exact
moment it was beaten,
left for dead.

Through this broken
looking glass, I see
a strong warrior
staring back at me.
No, this simply
cannot be.
This gladiator
cannot be me.

Oh, but she has fought,
and she has won
another battle,
another war.
She keeps on going,
unsafe from harm,
and unafraid
of the storms
that she will
find herself in,
knowing she will
continue to win.
She needs no hero,
as the princess
will save herself
again.

Haunted Lullabies

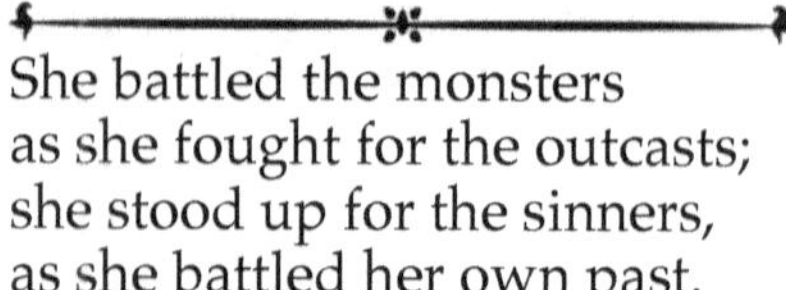

She battled the monsters
as she fought for the outcasts;
she stood up for the sinners,
as she battled her own past.

She walked into
the wicked woods,
walked out stronger
knowing her worth.

She sent her arrows flying
into evil hearts,
as she healed her wounds
and concealed her scars.

She went hungry
a time or two,
but still gave to others
who needed it more than her.

She stared into faces
who dared do her harm,
and cared deeply for
strangers' young.

She stitched up the cuts
that continued to bleed,
and headed back out
to the streets

to fight more battles,
for she does not know defeat;
she is everything I could wish
for her to be.

The Princess and Her Power

Ariel envied humans on land
and Alice was a dreamer.
Cinderella ached for nurturing,
and Belle, the avid reader.

Snow White built her family
amongst the animals and dwarfs;
Rapunzel yearned for freedom,
stuck in her tower without doors.

Sleeping Beauty was only
seeking out the truth;
when evil interrupted her
and imprisoned her to her bed of doom.

Tinkerbell believed in magic
and adventuring on the wind;
Jasmine stood for honor,
and helping all the land.

Anna was devoted
to her sister, the Queen,
even when Elsa was uncertain
of her power, not gleaned.

And all of these women
were expected to be saved
by someone more worthy,
someone more brave.

In all of these stories,
there is an evil villain
who must be stopped
to save the women.

But in this story,
she saves herself,
puts the glass shoe
back on the shelf.

She doesn't need
a magic carpet ride
to experience adventure
or to save her life.

She will not let anyone
steal her voice—
not Ursula,
and certainly not boys.

She can build her own library,
define her own tower,
face down her beasts,
control her own power.

She does not need the title
of princess or queen;
she creates her own story,
writes her own scenes.

She is but a woman—
not of royal blood;
she doesn't need a Prince Charming
to know and give love.

Fairy Goddess Mother

We get lost in our chores
and the things we aren't doing well,
too focused on errands and bills,
and so we dwell
on all of the mishaps,
on all of our faults;
we don't spend enough time
achieving what we want.
We mention—in passing—
all of our dreams,
not truly believing
they will come to be,
as there is no time
to devote to ourselves
when capitalist obligations
demand we buy what they sell.

Inside my head
and onto the pages,
I keep dreaming up worlds
where we can all be the greatest
versions of ourselves—
where peace resides,
where freedom dwells.

If I could pull a genie
from the lamp,
find a magic carpet
to fly us around,
pull the sword
from the stone,
or simply feed
all the hungry children,
then I would do so
with a wave of my wand.

I would not place limits
onto our wishes—
the strike of midnight
would mean absolutely nothing,
because abundance would be
overflowing to the poor,
as the rich get weak.

All the biggest dreams
of every little girl
would be granted in an instance.
They would not fear
to walk alone
or to fend off evil villains.

Women would rule,
and only the kindest of men—
not the ones who claim they're *nice*—
it's impossible to believe them.

Little boys would be taught
when a girl says "no"
to respect her boundaries
and leave her alone.

Evil, rich monsters
would be slayed by warriors—
women coming
to claim their vengeance.

And all of the good
put into the world
would be felt and shared
across the globe.

Billionaires would be non-existent,
wealth spread out when limits hit.
No more getting rich off of *our* labor,
caring for all of the innocent.

A fantasy world fills up my mind,
as I draft the words I seek to find
to keep a little bit of hope alive;
that is how I fill up my free time.

And maybe one day, it can truly be—
a place where all people *are* free,
not the hunger, the longing, the ache;
a real pumpkin carriage kind of place.

Of all of the wishes I have ever wished,
I believe I was born for this—
to become the fairy goddess mother
within the stories where we all seek comfort.

New Moon Offering

I release you.
I release the expectations.
I release the guilt.
I release the burdens
I have put on myself.
I release the regret.
I release the pain.
With this new moon,
I become whole again.
I release the worry.
I release the strife.
I release the angst
of this mortal life.
I do not follow
society's standards.
I do not accept
strangers' reprimanding.
I choose my path
in my own way.
I choose friends—
and family—
who *want* to stay.
I accept no judgement
or unsolicited opinions.
I release the fear
that I won't fit in.
I belong right where
I am.
I release the tension
bound in my hands.
I release you, worry.
I release you, doubt.
I do not have to have
the world figured out.
I release you, anger.
I release you, fear.
I do not have to carry
the weight of things
that are not even here.

I release the remorse,
the shame, and the sins.
I ask no god for
eternal forgiveness.
I do not need to repent
for all my wrongdoings.
I am but human,
and for that, I am worthy.
I release the pressure
that has been holding
me down.
I release the trauma
that has followed me around.
I release it all—
back to the wind.
I open myself up
to the Universe's gifts.
With this new moon,
I will rise.
I am not meant to suffer
through this life.
I accept the blessings.
I accept the love bestowed.
I ask for peace—
within me—to hold.

"As within, so without,
as above, so below,
as the universe, so the soul".
-*Hermetic Philosophy*

Time Bomb

Today, I am older
than you ever were;
I have breathed more breaths,
said more words,
traveled more steps,
and lived more life.

I realize,
with all this wisdom from age—
yes, that is a joke by the way—
that you didn't have time
to figure it all out.

As I am now older than you,
I have no doubt,
in time, you would have
figured it out.

You left broken pieces
splattered on the doors,
seeped into the walls,
your boots no longer
walking the floors.

And we were just expected to
go on living
forever
without you.

But people do it every day,
they say goodbye too soon,
and it's too late
to say the words
we held in too long,
to fix the problems,
to right the wrongs.

There is much to grieve
when a loved one is gone.

The pictures we never
got to take,
the memories we weren't
allowed to make,
the sorries we chose
not to say,
the grudges that got
in forgiveness's way.

Now that I am older
than you,
I find myself becoming
someone new…

and I believe you would have, too.

Death is a thief,
stealing our time,
no longer yours,
no longer mine.

Time is also a wise old friend,
showing us realities
we couldn't see back then—

before we aged and grew and learned
that life is messy, chaotic, and often
a burden.

It is the end we all receive;
though I miss you,
I am also relieved.

I believe my fire
would have enflamed yours;
you wouldn't have tamed me
forevermore.

As a girl, I was hypnotized
when I thought that grown-ups
were always right.

It took more time
to learn more lessons,
and the time I have left
is feeling lessened.

Though I may now
be older than you,
time has taught me
we often don't know
the right thing to do.

And with this time
that I have left,
I plan to forgive—
and maybe one day
forget.

Time is fleeting,
death always around the bend;
only time can tell
how my story will end.

Connection

It's amazing what a thought can bring—a fleeting moment, a memory.

I think of them, and in an instant, there they are, right beside me.

I feel wrapped up in a hug, when they join me in my thoughts,

as if no time has passed at all, and they've been beside me all along.

They really, truly never left.

They are buried in my soul, my chest.

Connected through the magic of the Universe.

Cravings

All my life
I have never felt
valued by a man.

Wanted.
Lusted for.
Craved.
Never valued.

I have given
all of me
to men
who never
saw me.

I have whittled myself
down
to the smallest fiber,
the smallest shaving
simply
to be
allowed.

Only to be left, craving.

Only for men
to trample
on my soul.

The footprints
of their lust,
their desire,
their cravings
etched into
my bones,
seeping into
my marrow.

There I was,
an innocent woman,
naivety telling me
fairytales are real.

And so,
I became
the princess
they wanted;
the one who
so desperately
yearned
to be saved.

This is what I craved.

They craved my body,
they craved the chants
from the other men
celebrating
a
successful
hunt.

I allowed them
to write my story,
edited
over and over
again.

I could never win.

They forget,
the princess
always feels
the pea;
she feels
what's there
underneath.

I chose them.
I chose
the lump
stuffed
into my bed;
not even a thousand
mattresses
could conceal it.

They sure thought
they were slick.

But that all changed
when I
finally
became
the vision
that *my* soul
craved.

The woman
who never
needed
to be saved.

Ripping away
the cloth,
the curtain,
the mask—
don't be a burden—
the expectations,
the fairytale,
the happy ending…

When I threw
away
the cravings.

My soul now craves
a different taste
upon my palate
within my space.

Trees of green
full of love,
peace within
and so above.

The women before me
guiding me there,
reminding me

that
cycles
break
here
with
me.

Finally feeling
fully me

just as
the
little
girl
inside
of me.

I *crave* peace.

Posthumously, Yours

As a child, I had a darker mind.
One I tucked away, locked up,
and tried to hide.
I had to be the very best—
student, daughter, sister,
guest.
Follow the rules,
say please and thank you.
Don't speak out or talk back,
don't voice your opinion.
I tried to do all the right things,
but everywhere I went,
the darkness followed me.
I drank it away for a little while.
I played its games from time to time.
But mostly I kept it deep inside—
a monster I never allowed
into the light.
I thought my mind must be a bit broken—
who would dream of slaying men
and chewing on their bones?
What cute little girl
who loved all things pink,
could have thoughts that would make
grown men scream?
I truly thought something
was wrong with me.
But those darker minds
inside the sweetest souls
make for chilling—and exciting—
stories to be told.
It only seemed appropriate
to publish them posthumously…
though, I'm not dead yet.

In Another Life

I keep writing these words that tell of a grim future, were you to live.

My fire enflaming yours, and you no longer able to tame me.

Though, I see that was quite unfair of me.

It is also quite possible that we would be
the greatest friends who always laugh, and you always swooping in
to save me again.

Why has it been so hard for me to envision a future where we could be
a bonded pair of silly weirdos,
learning together as we both grow old?

It is past time for me to let it all go—the thoughts that you'd be angry if I was no longer in your control.

You deserve a chance to be seen in the brightest light—all your good qualities.

And so, the gift I give to me (and to you), is the dream of a future where we both knew the other's flaws and secrets and still choose to lean on each other, to be silly together, to always forgive, and respect one another.

In another dimension, in another life, we are dancing and laughing by each other's side.

Can't Go Back to Yesterday

I finally found her!
It took long enough.
I searched on top mountains
and beneath the dirt.
I traveled far,
I traveled wide,
I kept seeking
as she would hide.
I looked to too many
unworthy men
to see if I could
find her again.
Of course, I now realize
that was quite mad in hindsight.

I walked through the strange,
the dark, and the bleak,
thinking she could be found
in strangers I'd meet.
That spark would return
of that little, lost girl,
and I could finally live
in my own dream world.

I stumbled upon vicious villains,
promising I would never have children
with any man who can't even be
the partner I need him to be.
And so, I focused all on me.

I forgot her whimsy,
forgot her innocence,
her love for stickers,
her love for writing.

And the entire time, I had it all trapped right here inside me!

It may sound silly,
not knowing I held
all of her
inside my head,
but there were too many
dark grey clouds;
she was lost to me
in a chaotic storm.

And so I searched inside of drinks,
inside of men I let in my bed;
I searched and searched—endlessly,
never giving up on finding her again.

And while I cannot go back to yesterday,
I can move forward with her next to me,
holding my hand and reminding me
that life is fleeting, and we need to all play
a little bit more, making silly jokes,
swinging on swings, jumping ropes—
though my bones are a bit weaker,
she reminds me that the grass is always greener
where you water it and help it to grow.
And I am never, ever truly alone.

While I was a very different person then,
I will never be her fully again,
but I'm finding her and letting her become
the woman I am so proud of.

Finding Alice

I am no longer scared
I am no longer weak;
I have fought demons at home
and out in the street.

I have carried the weight
of a thousand men
who tried to use me up
and get me to bow to them.

I have climbed mountains
and faced my own fears.
I have slayed dragons
and made friends with bears.

I smoked with a caterpillar
and made deals with a cat,
smiling at me from a tree
as we had a mad chat.

I dined with my enemies—
they were all so mad
when they couldn't turn me into
someone they could have.

I faced the Queen
who demanded my head,
then discovered that she
was also fed up with men.

I discovered within me
my very own power.
I learned to stand tall
and never to cower.

I followed some rabbits
into a dark hole,
came out on the other side
more quirky and bold.

At times, I felt small—
like a tiny ant.
But I brewed the potion
that helped me grow again.

I learned the lessons,
I showed forgiveness.
I promised myself
it was okay to be different.

I said goodbye to the people
who were holding me back,
and sought out the companions
who held power I lacked.

My story is not much different
than other tales.
It starts with confusion and worry,
where strange characters dwell.

Some may choose to stay right there,
in the beginning, without a care.

But Alice (I) chose to press on,
to see myself through the storm.

I entertained folks
who drove me right mad.
And learned that most witches
are not at all bad.

I have met the most
peculiar people—
who became my family,
who became my equals.

Having tea with strangers
and delicious cakes,
while little white rabbits
hop all over the place

reminding me that time is near;
we do not get enough time here.

While I know one day I must leave
and crawl back outside of this tree,
I am grateful for the lessons learned,
the love I gave, the love I earned.

This journey we're on
is meant to show us
that finding joy in life
should be our purpose.

No one can guide you—
not a white rabbit or cat.
You must find yourself.
That is just that.

· · — · ✳ · — · ·

"I can't go back to yesterday, because I was a different person
then."
- Lewis Carroll, *Alice's Adventures in Wonderland*

Goodbye for now

Life is surreal. One minute you're picking dandelions and making wishes, doing somersaults in the grass and tumbling down as you laugh and laugh. Next thing you know, you're building a life that you hope others will be inspired by. And then, like a ton of bricks, reality sets in and you're just working your life away, an endless cycle you repeat again and again. And all this time you lose loved ones, animals, and friends. And you keep waking up to do it again and again.

Like in Alice's story, we all go through a similar reality—confusion, transition, maturity, and hopefully—eventually—finding our true selves. In this poetic adventure—and a slight retelling—my goal is to remind you that even though your path is your own, you are not alone. As with Alice, never stop seeking out knowledge and understanding; never stop helping those in need along the way; find your power and stand strongly within it; and always embrace who you are fully at your core. We are not meant to lie down and obey. Never, ever forget to slay!

And may the wonderland you create for yourself be one you never want to escape from.

Love each other.
Love yourself more.

♡ Amanda
(a.k.a. The Book Witch)

350

Bonus Ending

Witches in Wonderland

It is a spooky, unusual Unbirthday
when the witches all gather for tea,
settling around the table
as curious as can be.

The cats are all chatting
in the trees with the crows,
and rabbits are sprinting
so fast, yet so slow.

It is quite curious…no?

There is madness abound
as the tea is poured;
Cheshire smiles
are all adorned

onto the faces
of all of the witches,
as they scheme and plot
to steal the riches
from the greedy, evil kings;
witches have always been
quite good at these things.

Within their witchy wonderland,
their familiars nestle close to them,
as they chop off the heads
of the soldiers sent
to destroy them.

They cackle as they sip,
for witches enjoy
this utter nonsense.

It did start as wishful thinking—
their plan to bury the king,
but it has turned into a celebration
on his Unbirthday.

The cards are all stacked,
the deck has been shuffled,
as the witches enjoy dining
and eating their truffles.

They have stirred up a dreamland
with their potions and brews.
They have designed a fairytale
to plant in their own storybooks.

Though their story
may have been banned
from all of the people
across all of the land,

they send out their rabbit
to lure in the children
who will sit at their table
and join them for dinner.

For adventures are exciting
when you're just a child,
and though this isn't Neverland,
your young heart can go wild.

They have sent their invitations
and set the hourglass,
enjoying all the chatter
as the time is passed.

And when they see
that mile-wide grin
from their maddest cat,

they know it's time to journey out,
and they adorn the mad witch's hat.

Of course, the rabbit is late again,
he's a bit mad too;
so, they shall meet him at the hole
he's always climbing through.

Though it does not matter
which way they go,
many paths will take them there;

their resilience and curiosity
will lead them to the king's lair.

With a little imagination—
and a few strands of his hair—
the witches of wonderland
will ensure the king's despair.

Dark has fallen
and the moon is alive,
guiding their way as
they march through the night.

The Queen is waiting
when they arrive,
as she's part of the plan
they have contrived.

She is ready to sneak them into
the parlor where the king is waiting.

The witches know the importance
of accepting your true self,
and basking in the quirkiness
that we all have felt.

And this king, he never knew
who he truly was;
he always forced others
to do his bidding and such stuff.

He sent soldiers to battle
wars that weren't theirs,
even those nonexistent
where the kingdom's people lived.

He scooped up all of their food
and all of their coins—
stuffed in his pockets,
and now the people will join

all of the witches as they move in,
prepared to chop off some heads—
with the Queen leading them.

This fairytale does have a happy ending,
though not the kind that includes
a princess who needed saving.

The people will cheer
and write it into their history—
"The king is dead!"

Oh, but *how* is still a mystery…

The witches have entered
the royal palace,
swearing secrecy for how
they deal their malice.

They shuffled their deck,
they let the cards fall;
and the witches will reign
once and for all.

To be continued…

Final Bonus Ending

Saving Alice

It started as an escape—
a place to disappear to
where I could dream,
believe, be.

Like a long lost friend, it called to me.

The paper. The ink.

Drowning in words
inside my head,
slipping into a fantasy
as I wrote in my bed.

A dream land where
daddies never die,
where animals never starve,
where true love waits.

And then I began to live a different fate.

I lost my words. I lost my faith.

I left it behind
for far too long,
keeping it all trapped
within my mind.

Filled with stories
never told,
with words of wisdom,
and tales of woe.

And finally,
there it was
waiting for me
to pick it back up.

So I poured it all
onto the page,
splashing and slashing,
releasing all the rage.

And as the words spilled out,
the tears did too—
all the weight I had carried
had been let loose.

A heavy burden finally reduced.

And now I am writing
the tales I wish to read,
of women fighting back,
taking down greed.

I'm inspiring myself
with my own words,
wishing so desperately
that I could have heard

these same stories
when I was so young;
maybe then I wouldn't
have chased men so long.

I am finding comfort
and utter peace
alone at home
where I don't need

anyone to rescue me;
inside my solace,
I have built a wealth
of knowledge.

Books and words
have always saved me;
I could slip away and
enjoy the beauty

within a world
I could not see—
imagination the superpower
inside of me.

And if my words
one day find you,
I truly hope
they can save you, too.

Final Final Bonus Ending

Forbidden Fairytale

Goldilocks found a home
of which she did not own;
still, she walked right inside
no idea what she'd find.

Fresh food there
right on the stove,
one too hot,
one too cold.

Lured into a
necessary slumber
after curing her
aching hunger.

No place of her own
to get some rest
out of the cold,
out of the wet.

She only wanted
a moment to forget
her burdened life,
her unfair hand.

But the powers that be
claimed her a monster
for taking food
to feed her hunger,

for sitting in
a broken chair
to rest the feet
that brought her there.

Then claiming her
responsible
for all the damage
done to her.

Goldilocks had
not a penny
to her name,
her pockets empty.

And all the bears,
they hoarded it all—
the food, the shelter,
the coin, the laws.

All that was left for Goldilocks—
and all the little piggies—
was to fight amongst themselves,
pointing fingers at each other.

And the rich fucking cowards
remained inside
allowing the helpless
to die outside.

Until one day
Goldi formed a plan,
to trick the bears
off the land.

They plotted for hundreds
of days and nights,
taking their time,
getting it right.

Unlike the Trojans
scheming for a day,
this plan needed
time to bake.

And when it was
finally time,
they rose up
against their crimes.

As some fell,
others rose strong,
and the poorly citizens
proved them wrong.

Stacked in numbers,
millions deep,
they discovered the power
the rich wanted to keep.

As the castle
tumbled down,
the people stood
on even ground.

Without their walls
they had no strength;
their gold could no longer
keep them safe.

As the people moved in
for the kill,
a queen arose
with a new will.

As the fire
burned it down
and ashes settled
on the ground,

a new kingdom was formed—
not run by rich, evil men—
and the fearless women
took control of them.

These stories are not
the fairytales of our youth—
those meant to scare us
into *their* rules.

These are the stories
that they banned
from all the children
across all the land.

These stories were taken
and rearranged
to fit *their* agenda
so women could be blamed.

But the curse has lifted;
we've been set free.
It is time to reign
in the matriarchy.

The End. (for now)

More *Forbidden Fairytales* are coming…

Amanda L. Ball

A Closing Dedication

A Winter Storm

It burns inside of me.

What started as an ember
has sparked and emblazoned
an inferno full of fury,
full of empathy and anger.

Snow began falling
atop of my flames,
as if I don't have a right
to feel all this rage.

The screams of the innocent
rang through the ears
of all of the people
full of sadness and fear,

bundled in layers
and bundled in love
for all of the victims
they keep taking from us.

Holding our phones
to record their misdeeds,
they continue to kill
even as people flee.

As night fell upon us
and blood seeped into the streets,
the people kept marching
on worn, tired feet.

The sun is going down
and the snow will all freeze,
but the people refuse to ever
admit defeat.

They shoot us down
and we continue to rise.
So, let the storm come,
we aren't hiding inside.

We all know that fire
can melt all the ice.

To all of the victims of I.C.E. and a broken, unjust system. May
all the beautiful souls taken rest in eternal peace. May every
human one day know the freedom we all deserve. ♡

About the Author

Amanda L. Ball has been writing poetry since she was a young girl, having her first poem published in a book for young poets at age 11. It has been her lifelong dream to publish her own collection of poetry. She is a loud, relentless voice for social justice and cares deeply about child and animal welfare.

Though she grew up and lived in Texas for 35 years, she has spent time traveling the world, living as a nomad across the country, and currently resides in the state of Maryland with her cats, enjoying her passion for books and writing, and reveling in the middle-aged friendships she has discovered, grown, and continues to nurture every day.

And she has never stopped dreaming.

Other Works by the Author:
Storm of Enchanted Dreams: a poetic fairytale (second edition)
Wicked Dreams Goodnight: a witchy fairytale

Follow the author on social media: *@echoendlessmind*

www.ingramcontent.com/pod-product-compliance
Lightning Source LLC
Chambersburg PA
CBHW071727150726
47998CB00005B/1543